W9-BTL-927

When You Need a
Miracle

The Seven Secrets of Faith

When You Need a
Miracle

The Seven Secrets of Faith

CHERIE HILL

Waterfall
PRESS

(References are continued on p. 87 and constitute a continuation of the copyright page.)

To Bret Mischlich,

"God knew."

Every day is a miracle with you in it.
And you're right,
"God's grace is ALWAYS amazing."

CONTENTS

CHAPTER 1
You're Right Where God Wants You 1

CHAPTER 2
Seek God's Will More than Your Own 23

CHAPTER 3
Keep Your Eyes on God 41

CHAPTER 4
Turn Your Fear into Faith 53

CHAPTER 5
Trust God, No Matter What 63

CHAPTER 6
See Your Trial as God Does 75

CHAPTER 7
Praise God for the Past, Present, and Future 87

1

YOU'RE RIGHT WHERE GOD WANTS YOU

Life has a way of bringing you to places where there's nowhere to run and no place to hide—where fear not only consumes you, but paralyzes you. Minutes slip away and life seems to effortlessly lose its meaning as you pray for a way out of the desperation that consumes your soul. And you thought you understood emptiness, until your life fell apart and your spirit bottomed out—beyond the limits you thought emptiness had. You're not even sure what it is you're holding on to anymore—the pain is consuming you from the inside out, but, for some reason, in your brokenness, you're hanging out to see if faith works. Even when nothing is *adding up* and *giving up* seems to be the only option, you step into another day, another hour, another minute, holding on just in case God shows up—hoping that life doesn't unravel and your heart doesn't cave in—because *life is wearing thin.*

As you struggle to trust God, when you need Him the most, to *provide a way out*, you find that God's plans are taking you on a different route: straight *through*. And that's not what you were hoping for. Though you were convinced you were walking in faith, what faith you thought you had has now given way to hopelessness, and you're not sure that you ever had faith at all.

Discouragement can take over when you were counting on your faith to work in a time like this. It's all but failing you in the moment you need it most—if God doesn't show up, *it's all over*. Everything hinges upon Him making His presence and power evident in ways that seem *beyond* impossible. And it's in your desperation and despair that you realize there's one thing you need: *a miracle*.

Through prolonged periods of pain, pressure, and circumstances that press us into impossibilities, we can find ourselves trapped, hurting, and overcome with a hopelessness that grabs such a hold of us that even if there *were* a "*way of escape*," we wouldn't have the strength to *see* it or *take* it (1 Corinthians 10:13).

As we struggle to take just one more step of faith, we find that the hardest part of trusting God is realizing that through life's darkest valleys, God has either led us into our impossible place, or allowed us to wander there for reasons that may never be revealed to anyone other than Him. And we're just not sure we can live with that ... because *time* and *pain* can take its toll on our soul, and at some point, *we need to be delivered*.

We need to experience God in our circumstances to the extent that we'll never forget His presence, power, and sovereignty as we journey through the rest of life. We need that kind of faith—but sometimes it takes time, and we're consumed with the reality that time is *not* on our side. And even if it were, it's the waiting that drives us into places of despair that we never knew existed.

When faith demands our patience and we're waiting on God to reveal Himself in earthshaking ways in our lives, God's *delays* appear to be His *denials. But they are not.* God's ways take us into places where we'll question His existence and demand proof of it—desperation drives us to the only One who can pull us out of our pit of despair (Psalm 40:2). And sometimes that pit is so *deep* and so *dark* that it seems we'll never see the light of day.

If you're facing insurmountable circumstances, surrounded by impossibilities, you're in a *"Red Sea"* moment. And even if you're not in one right now, you can rest assured you will be. *It's only a matter of time.*

Red Sea moments take us back to the biblical book of Exodus, where God, in history-making fashion, proved that He will make a way when there seems to be no way. The Red Sea moment in Exodus provides us God's method of how to turn our *fear into faith* and *problems into praise.* And when we're overwhelmed and uncertain of God's power and presence in the midst of our impossible situations in life, we need to be reminded that God is with us ... to deliver us ... in His perfect way ... in His impeccable timing.

We can find hope in our Red Sea moments by fully grasping the miracle done there, as our own Red Sea rages before us, with a desert entrapping us and the enemy bearing down with each passing minute. In that moment, although we look back and see a past that *we can't live with* and a future we're not sure *we'll live through,* we can look up to a God who works in the unseen. Though it seems like nothing is happening, God is orchestrating every detail of our miracle, and He's well aware that we desperately need our *faith to take sight.*

As we seek God's face and are desperate for His hand, it's in the most hopeless moments of our lives that we learn that the hardest part of pain and suffering is the ingredient of *time.* Know that, throughout life, you'll experience short, sharp pangs that come and go with little long-lasting effect ... and they will take their toll on your soul. Know that it's when you experience suffering that lingers—drags you through long, monotonous years, returning day after day with the same hopeless agony—that your spirit can lose its strength and God's grace will be the *only* thing that will keep you from sinking into the abyss of despair.

Though it's often difficult to see God's hand, much less glimpse His plan, it's His heart you can trust as faith assures you He's on His throne, calmly awaiting the moment when He will open the gates of heaven and His glory will pour out.

"The Lord will make a way for you where no foot has been before. That which, like a sea, threatens to drown you, shall be a highway for your escape." —Charles H. Spurgeon

But in the meantime, *time* serves its purpose, because until that moment when God displays His truth that *"all things work together for good"* in your life (Romans 8:28), you will remain in a place of being anxious for the hour of your deliverance ... and believe it or not, *that's right where God wants you.*

It's when we're most anxious and extraordinarily distressed that God steps into our lives in an earthshaking way, *even as our world seems to be falling apart.* And realize that that point of no return may be a lot further than you hoped it was. God will hold our faith to the fire to refine it, and He may heat the fire to such a degree that you're certain He's out to *destroy* you, not *perfect* you (Malachi 3:3).

God's ways go far beyond our understanding of them, and when we're looking for a miracle, desperate for God to make a way through impossible situations, we need to rest assured that God specializes in making a way when there appears to be no way. He longs to reveal Himself to you *more* than you desire to have Him do so.

But recognizing God takes faith. Mountains don't move and Red Seas can never be parted without it. If we take into account God's almighty presence, power, providence, and unfailing promises, we can go through our pain and suffering in that light—faith changes *everything*. And there are two things you should know: God can do ANYTHING and prayer changes EVERYTHING.

You might be facing a Red Sea or entrapped in a desert; you might be consumed with fear from an encroaching enemy and you may be looking back at all that you've endured, knowing you must go forward, but overtaken and paralyzed with the fear of a future that looks impossible. You can spend countless hours trying desperately not to remember all that you can't forget, and as you try to grasp the reality of it all, there appears to be no way *out* and you're certain you'll never make it *through*. But God works in *unseen* ways. His way of escape *will* come, but it may come in the way of a miracle you could have never anticipated—don't underestimate God's abilities, nor His love for you. *His grace will be more than enough when you're desperate for a loan on faith.* And rest assured, God WILL make a way for you—He's promised He will:

> *"I will even make a way in the wilderness, and rivers in the desert."* (Isaiah 43:19 KJV)

> *"When you pray, keep alert and be thankful. Be sure to pray that God will make a way."* (Colossians 4:2–3 CEV)

> *"The LORD will utterly ... make a way to cross on foot."* (Isaiah 11:15 NRSV)

God will do whatever it takes to split Red Seas and move mountains *when He finds faith that believes he will.*

"Since ancient times no one has heard, no ear has perceived, no eye has seen any God besides you, who acts on behalf of those who wait for him." (Isaiah 64:4 NIV)

"The LORD's eyes scan the whole world to find those whose hearts are committed to him and to strengthen them." (2 Chronicles 16:9 GOD'S WORD)

You may not realize that you're at a Red Sea, but your circumstances say you are, and you need to understand how the Israelites got through their Red Sea moment *if you're to make it through your own.* As you take your own journey, remember that miracles happen in moments like these—when you're trapped by circumstances, full of fear, facing impossible odds, and desperate for God to show up … it's the perfect setup for a *miracle.*

If we go back and take a look at how this miracle came about, we find, in the biblical book of Exodus, Israelite slaves suffering, well over fifty years, under the hand of Pharaoh—with no hope in sight. But after God sent devastating plagues upon Pharaoh and Egypt, and called upon Moses to lead his people out of captivity, the Israelites found themselves faced with the Red Sea. They were free, but trapped—with six hundred of Pharaoh's best chariots and a massive army closing in to end their lives. They were trapped with mountains on one side and a Red Sea in front of them. Fear consumed them as they declared they'd rather be slaves again than to die in the desert:

"What have you done to us by bringing us out of Egypt?" (Exodus 14:11 NIV)

We can often find ourselves in the same place. In fact, as we've stepped out in faith, trusting in God, we find ourselves filled with more fear and doubt, and we didn't think faith was supposed to work that way. But God uses Moses to speak strength, hope, and a powerful promise to the Israelites. This promise is for you, too, in your Red Sea moments:

> "Moses answered the people, 'Do not be afraid. Stand firm and you will see the deliverance the Lord will bring you today. The Egyptians you see today you will never see again. The Lord will fight for you; you need only to be still.'" (Exodus 14:13–14, NIV)

God was with them, and He's with *you*, too. It may not seem like you're where God wants you to be, but you are. And whether you realize it or not, you are *constantly* under the *covering* of God's grace—there is nothing to fear. He is with you *always*.

In Exodus, the angel of God was in a pillar of cloud, standing between the people and the Egyptians, protecting them. And it was in that moment, even in their paralyzing fear, that He worked the miracle. Moses stretched his hand out over the sea and caused a strong east wind to blow all night, parting the waters and transforming the seafloor into dry land.

Realize that this wasn't the miracle the Israelites were *expecting*—your miracle won't be what you're *expecting* either. In fact, many times God begins to part the Red Seas in our life; He starts moving mountains, and *we doubt the miracle*. We *believe* and then end up in *disbelief*. We need to clearly understand that God's ways, being far above our own, bring about miracles that may come in a way that drives us into deeper despair—your miracle may cause you to question God in more ways than you ever imagined. But don't allow your faith to walk by sight— that's not the way faith works. It was during the night when the Israelites fled through the Red Sea—*not the ideal situation*.

When you're afraid, darkness doesn't help the situation. Fear brings with it its own kind of darkness. But even in the darkness, we must trust that God is at work—there are *no* coincidences.

"There are no coincidences in God's providence."
—Cindy Woodsmall, *A Season for Tending*

It's evident that the miracle at the Red Sea was no coincidence. (It's been said, "coincidences are God's way of remaining anonymous.") Be assured, it's God who will work your miracle, and it may be in your *darkest day* and *longest night*.

As you pray for your miracle, know that God isn't looking for a perfect heart, but simply one that seeks after His—so seek Him *always*, especially in your moments of despair ... because believe it or not, He's with you *in those very moments*. When a cloud of darkness covers you, and you're convinced that God has abandoned you, know that God is with you *always* (Matthew 28:20) and is aware of every tear you shed—He bottles each one (Psalm 56:8).

As difficult as it is to accept, the pain and suffering you're going through is *observed* and often *ordered*, while fully permitted by God Himself. And there's no need to worry. God's got *every* detail covered. We don't want to ever put question marks where God has put periods.

"Worry is putting question marks where God has put periods."
—John R. Rice

Worry should be the catalyst for prayer and fear should be the driving force that escalates our faith. *We've got to stop trying to worry our way out of our despair.*

"The beginning of anxiety is the end of faith, and the beginning of true faith is the end of anxiety." —George Müller

Uncertainty, the countless unknowns in life, should drive us to the throne of God. Within *every* moment we feel trapped and overwhelmed, we should find ourselves relentlessly trusting in God's promises, regardless of our circumstances that seem to contradict them. We need to clearly understand that our Red Sea moments are what God uses to test our faith, teach us wisdom, and show us His ways. You might not know what your future holds, *but God does* ... and you can trust Him to lead and guide you for His name's sake.

> *"He guides me in paths of righteousness for his name's sake."*
> (Psalm 23:3 NIV)

God's vision is clear, His promises precise, and His love unfailing—walk by faith when your vision is distorted through your pain and suffering. Know that God knows *where you are* and *how to get you where He wants you to be*—in His glory.

> *"'He knows the way He taketh,' even if for the moment we do not."*—J. I. Packer

You're no different than the Israelites in the book of Exodus. They faced a Red Sea where nothing but a miracle could save them—*at some point you will, too.* Their story is *your* story. Their miracle will be similar to your own. The Exodus account wasn't written for them, it was written for *you.* In the *very* situation you're in ... if you can apply it, you'll find a miracle within it, and your life will never be the same. It's realizing that whoever you are, wherever you are, and whatever you're going through, God will deliver you. *But it takes faith.* And the Red Sea moments, *when nothing but a miracle will do,* are the places where you'll experience God in greater ways than you can fathom. Faith will bring you face to face with God Almighty, and you, not unlike Moses, will get a glimpse of God's glory. That's what happens at Red Sea moments in life ... so brace yourself for a miracle of all miracles. But know this: as you declare your faith, *it will be tested* ... because faith is not faith *until it's tested.* Your Red Sea will become the element of your faith. Embrace your fear by standing firm in your faith … *that's when miracles happen.*

> *"Israel had been brought into the present predicament by God Himself. It was the Pillar of Cloud which had led them to where they were now encamped. Important truth for us to lay hold of. We must not expect the path of faith to be an easy and smooth one. Faith must be tested, tested severely. But why? That we may learn the sufficiency of our God! That we may prove from experience that He is able to supply our every need (Philippians 4:19), and make a way of escape from every temptation (1 Corinthians 10:13), and do for us exceedingly abundantly above all that we ask or think."* —A. W. Pink, *Gleanings in Exodus*

We need to grasp the truth about our trial … it's a test, *it's only a test.* And the test isn't about passing or failing—the Israelites continually failed, miserably—it's about experiencing the fullness of God's glory and receiving His grace when you least deserve it and would never expect it. Faith brings us into a right relationship with God and gives Him the opportunity to work within our lives, drawing us nearer to Him so that He might fully reveal Himself to us in ways we never imagined. But all too often, in order for Him to do that, He must knock the bottom out of our faith, time and time again, in order to draw our attention back to Him. He wants us to understand that it is a *life* of faith, not a faith that is centered around a single event or an experience of great blessings. Faith is a *journey*, not a *destination.*

So, your Red Sea moments, when the impossibilities in your circumstances flood out any faith you thought you had, are what will prove your faith and develop your unshakable trust in God. And though it seems hard to believe now, your sea *will* part, and these words will *haunt* and *overwhelm your spirit with joy* at the same time:

> *"Did I not tell you that if you believed, you would see the glory of God?"* (John 11:40 NIV)

It's faith that rolls back the floodwaters and dries up the ground on which you'll walk as you experience God in your life like never before.

> *"Faith is a footbridge that you don't know will hold you up over the chasm until you're forced to walk out on it."* —Nicholas Wolterstorff

Here's the key: don't try to bridge your Red Sea. Leave room for God to work a miracle. Expect the miracle, but let go of your expectations about the details of it. In your hopelessness, give way to full surrender and realize that God is far bigger than you are. When it seems as though a miracle occurring in your life is impossible, realize, fully, that it is—*that's why it's a miracle*. If the situation you're facing weren't impossible, you wouldn't need *a miracle*.

The very definition of a miracle, according to Merriam-Webster's online dictionary, points *only* to God: *"an unusual or wonderful event that is believed to be caused by the power of God."* So don't be surprised by your situation. If you're desperate for a miracle, the truth is *you're desperate for God*. And that may very well be the whole reason for God allowing the circumstances that have driven you to such a desperate place.

You may doubt that God *can* or *will* show up, but you can rest assured that behind every miracle there are two words that always follow: *"but God."* No matter the situation, beyond all the doubt, there's always a *but God*.

"Once you were dead because of your disobedience and your many sins. You used to live in sin, just like the rest of the world, obeying the devil—the commander of the powers in the unseen world. He is the spirit at work in the hearts of those who refuse to obey God. All of us used to live that way, following the passionate desires and inclinations of our sinful nature. By our very nature we were subject to God's anger, just like everyone else.

*"**But God** is so rich in mercy, and he loved us so much, that even though we were dead because of our sins, he gave us life when he raised Christ from the dead. (It is only by God's grace that you have been saved!) For he raised us from the dead along with Christ and seated us with him in the heavenly realms because we are united with Christ Jesus. So God can point to us in all future ages as examples of the incredible wealth of his grace and kindness toward us, as shown in all he has done for us who are united with Christ Jesus."* (Ephesians 2:1–7 NLT; emphasis mine)

We mess up. Life gets hard and choices take us down paths we never wanted to go. *But God* doesn't move ... and His love *never* changes. He's the same yesterday, today, and *forever* (Hebrews 13:8). And He's the God of miracles *when you're in desperate need of them.*

"'No chance at all,' Jesus said, 'if you think you can pull it off by yourself. Every chance in the world if you trust God to do it.'" (Luke 18:27 MSG)

"What is impossible for people is possible with God." (Luke 18:27 NLT)

You may not be able to see the "way" or the *possibility* of a miracle, **but God** does. So you're going to have to trust Him, *by faith.* And if we're to experience miracles in our lives, we need to clearly understand what it means to live "*by faith*," and why this Red Sea moment in Exodus is so vital to *our* faith walk—because our miracle will happen "*by faith*."

> "***By faith*** *they passed through the Red Sea as though they were passing through **dry land**; and the **Egyptians**, when they attempted it, **were drowned**.*" (Hebrews 11:29 NASB; emphasis mine)

If we need the pathway to a miracle paved in our lives, we're going to need to take an even deeper look into this miracle, in order to understand God's ways and how faith plays the vital part in bringing about the miracles we pray for. If we go back to the beginnings of this journey, to the Red Sea, we find Moses called God's people to apply the blood of the Passover lamb so that they might be delivered from the judgment that was to befall Egypt.

> "*It was **by faith** that Moses commanded the people of Israel to keep the Passover and to sprinkle blood on the doorposts so that the angel of death would not kill their firstborn sons.*" (Hebrews 11:28 NLT; emphasis mine)

Nothing happens with God except *by faith*. With faith, Moses led the people out of Egypt, eventually passing through the Red Sea. And although you'd think that being free of the bondage of slavery was enough of a miracle, God is setting the stage for greater miracles, even in the midst of the people's continued doubt and disbelief. *He'll do the same for you.* It doesn't take "much" faith. It's not about *quantity*, but *quality*. Small faith opens God's hand just as much as great faith does. *Faith is faith.*

> "*The Lord answered, 'If you had faith even as small as a mustard seed, you could say to this mulberry tree, "May you be uprooted and thrown into the sea," and it would obey you!'*" (Luke 17:6 NLT)

We've heard these words of Jesus countless times, and we know that the mustard seed is extraordinarily small, but what could we be missing about faith through this reference in His parable? We need to have a better understanding because Jesus's words were always *carefully chosen* and *fully packed* with powerful messages that cut right to the heart of the matter, breaking ground for miracles within our own heart.

First, we find that a mustard seed does not grow into a tree. Jesus told us in Mark 4:32 that the mustard seed is "greater than all herbs." Mustard is an herb that grows into a large shrub. It can reach a maximum height of eight feet (three meters), but still doesn't become a tree. It never becomes big enough for birds to lodge in it. Our faith may become "large," from our perspective, but to God, *all things are small.*

Second, we should understand that the mustard seed is *not* the smallest of seeds; there are many varieties of seeds smaller than the mustard seed. So even if our faith is as small as a mustard seed, we can find God's grace to help us understand that *it's enough.*

You see, it's not primarily the size of faith that was at the heart of Jesus's message here. It was the *property* of the seed that Jesus wanted to focus upon. If you open or dissect a mustard seed, you find that it's compact, with no air chamber in it—unlike most seeds. Air, symbolically, in the Bible, has been associated with evil and not with God (Ephesians 2:2). So this parable gives way to the idea that mustard-seed faith is *pure.*

So faith works, no matter its size, as long as it is pure, eliminating doubt and fear. And it's through the tests of life, in the Red Sea moments, where we get to assess our faith. Our tests aren't for God to take measure of our faith, they're for *our* benefit. *We* need to know where we stand in our faith. And Red

Sea moments quickly determine just where our faith stands. Because these moments bring about opportunities to fear and doubt like nothing does. We find God in our most desperate moments, when we believe the worst is behind us and there is nothing but blessings before us, taking us deeper in our faith than we ever thought we could go.

We want the easy route, the one of least resistance, *but faith never grows there.* So God sees fit to take us into desperate situations, dark valleys, where we face ultimate destruction.

> *"So God led them in a roundabout way through the wilderness toward the Red Sea."* (Exodus 13:18 NLT)

Though God may lead us on a journey we're not prepared to take, *He goes with us.* He guides and protects. He is *always* sovereign. He goes ahead of you, He knows, and when your miracle happens, remember that all along, *God knew.* He *knew* what you would face, He *knew* all of your fears and doubts that would threaten to drown your soul, He *knew* the despair you'd be tempted to give in to, He *knew* every detail, and He will use it all to bring about the miracle that will flood your spirit with greater awe and joy than you ever thought possible.

> *"The LORD went ahead of them. He guided them during the day with a pillar of cloud, and he provided light at night with a pillar of fire. This allowed them to travel by day or by night."* (Exodus 13:21 NLT)

It's *before* the miracle, when circumstances become insurmountable, and God's hands seem bound and His power limited, when you'll find your faith failing. But don't be deceived in your faith walk ... you're going to face the impossible before you ever see that *"with God all things are possible"* (Matthew 19:26).

"So the Egyptians pursued them, all the horses and chariots of Pharaoh, his horsemen and his army, and overtook them camping by the sea beside Pi Hahiroth, before Baal Zephon."
(Exodus 14:9 NKJV)

Camping—in the dark. It's those times when we need a miracle, and nothing seems to be happening, that we need to remember that God is fully aware of the miracles we'll need now *and* in the future. Let God be God and just believe that He's at work; allow Him to quiet your heart and simply rest in His grace. He's with you always and will never leave you nor forsake you (Matthew 28:20, Deuteronomy 31:6). But here's the thing: you'll *feel* like God has left you and forsaken you, and you'll completely doubt that He is with you *always*. That's what happens at Red Sea moments in life—*so expect it.*

You might be experiencing your darkest day, but God works in the night—He did at the Red Sea in Exodus and He will in your own life. It was during the night, *when it was dark*, that God worked the miracle ... they weren't sure what kind of miracle they needed, but *God knew*. And God worked the miracle by using a pillar of cloud to protect the Hebrews as He caused a strong east wind to blow all night, parting the waters and turning the seafloor into dry land. It was during the night that the Israelites walked through the Red Sea, the Egyptian army charging after them.

Grab hold of this: in the midst of the miracle, *it may not seem like one*. The miracle occurred, the Red Sea parted, but there was still an army charging after them. It didn't seem like much of a miracle as they remained consumed with fear at the *sight* of the circumstances—but faith doesn't walk by sight, because if it did, you'd think that when you're set free from the bondage of slavery, you wouldn't find yourself in another impossible situation, faced with peril—trapped between a sea and an army—not exactly what you'd expect when you're "delivered." The Israelites cried out to Moses on their journey, hoping God would hear, loud and clear:

> *"They said to Moses, 'Was it because there were no graves in Egypt that you brought us to the desert to die? What have you done to us by bringing us out of Egypt?'"* (Exodus 14:11 NIV)

What kind of God does this? Takes you out of one desperate situation, only to lead you into another? The God of *miracles*. Because the same God who leads you *in*, will lead you *out*:

"The Will of God"

The will of God will never take you,
Where the grace of God cannot keep you,
Where the arms of God cannot support you,
Where the riches of God cannot supply your needs,
Where the power of God cannot endow you.

The will of God will never take you,
Where the spirit of God cannot work through you,
Where the wisdom of God cannot teach you,
Where the army of God cannot protect you,
Where the hands of God cannot mold you.

The will of God will never take you,
Where the love of God cannot enfold you,
Where the mercies of God cannot sustain you,
Where the peace of God cannot calm your fears,
Where the authority of God cannot overrule for you.

The will of God will never take you,
Where the comfort of God cannot dry your tears,
Where the Word of God cannot feed you,

Where the miracles of God cannot be done for you,
Where the omnipresence of God cannot find you.

—Author: Unknown

In your Red Sea moment, you'll be overcome with fear. There's no question about that. But fear is the *doorway* to greater faith—it points you to God and opens the path for a miracle. When the Israelites were overtaken with fear, Moses pointed them to God—*fear has a way of doing that.*

> "And Moses said to the people, '**Do not be afraid. Stand still**, and see the salvation of the LORD, which He will accomplish for you today. For the Egyptians whom you see today, you shall see again no more forever.'" (Exodus 14:13 NKJV; emphasis mine)

It seems clear the people had *little* faith. But God *still* worked the miracle—don't forget that in your own life. You may feel that your faith has run out, that it's been drowned out by despair, **but God** sees your heart ... He's got a handle on your faith, *even when you don't.*

It looked as though the Israelites were crying out to God in anger, doubt, and disbelief, but God heard a *prayer.* A prayer that He demanded be followed by action—obedience to move forward at His command, *even in their fear.* Sometimes you have to take the next step of faith ... *afraid.*

> "The LORD said to Moses, 'Why do you cry to me? Tell the people of Israel to go forward.'" (Exodus 14:15 ESV)

God called the people to stop praying and take action. Sometimes our faith needs to move forward and trust God to provide the way, *even when it seems impossible that there is one.* And when God has prepared a path, even if all you can see is the very next step in front of you, *you'll need to move forward.* You'll need to obey God and have faith, *even in your doubt* ... because that's *when* and *where* miracles happen.

> *"Then Moses stretched out his hand over the sea; and the LORD caused the sea to go back by a strong east wind all that night, and made the sea into dry land, and the waters were divided. So the children of Israel went into the midst of the sea on the dry ground, and the waters were a wall to them on their right hand and on their left."* (Exodus 14:21–22 NKJV)

No matter how things appear, *never* let your faith walk by sight.

> *"And though He delayeth His help, and the evil seemeth to grow worse and worse, be not weak, but rather strong, and rejoice, since the most glorious promises of God are generally fulfilled in such a wondrous manner that He steps forth to save us at a time when there is the least appearance of it. He commonly brings His help in our greatest extremity, that His finger may plainly appear in our deliverance. And this method He chooses that we may not trust upon anything that we see or feel, as we are always apt to do, but only upon His bare Word, which we may depend upon in every state."*
> —C. H. Von Bogatsky

> *"Remember it is the very time for faith to work when sight ceases. The greater the difficulties, the easier for faith; as long as there remain certain natural prospects, faith does not get on even as easily as where natural prospects fail."*
> —George Müller

Your Red Sea moment is a test of your faith. If you need a miracle, *you'll need faith to believe it's "as good as done."* As long as you're waiting for the miracle, hoping for it, looking for evidence of it, you're not walking "by faith." You might be full of *hope*, but not *faith*. Because faith is the *"substance* of things hoped for, the *evidence* of things not seen" (Hebrews 11:1; emphasis mine).

Substance—something that exists.

Evidence—proof, something manifested.

True faith counts on God and believes *before* it sees. When we pray for a miracle, it's natural for us to want to see some evidence that our petition is granted before we stand firm in our belief, but when we're walking by faith, we need no evidence other than God's word.

> *"You get faith by studying the Word. Study that Word until something in you "knows that you know" and that you do not just hope that you know."* —Carrie Judd Montgomery

The faith that believes without seeing is what sustains us in our most trying places ... when the Red Sea is before us and the army is encroaching. *We need to believe in order to see.* The Psalmist reminds us:

> *"What, what would have become of me had I not believed that I would see the Lord's goodness in the land of the living!"* (Psalm 27:13 AMP)

We can see through impossibilities when we're looking at life through eyes of faith—it's then that we can watch with delight to see how God is going to make a path through the Red Sea, when there is no human way out of our circumstances. *The stage is being set* and *the curtain is about to be drawn.* And it's while we *wait* in anticipation that this time of testing grows our faith and strengthens it. Faith *must* be tested. And here's the *first secret* of faith, when you're faced with a Red Sea moment: *you're right where God wants you* because your faith is about to be tested ... and when your faith is tested, *miracles* follow.

2

SEEK GOD'S WILL MORE THAN YOUR OWN

It's been said time and time again, in the words of Woody Allen, *"If you want to make God laugh, tell Him your plans."* No doubt the Israelites had plans for their lives, and *so do we.* And *none* of those plans include severe testing of our faith, but faith can't be possessed without experiencing trials. *No one* has ever had faith without it being tested. We need our life's circumstances to drive us forward in our faith so that we will fully grasp that God's will is *always* best. We can't allow ourselves to be driven into despair when our faith is tested; because God's will always tests our faith—it's a matter of whether or not we'll embrace it—it's about seeking Him and His plans, *instead of our own.*

Red Sea moments cause us to question our faith like nothing else does. When there's no way of escape and only a miracle will do, our faith seems to be tested *beyond* its limits. But if we'll understand the purpose of the impossible situations in our lives, if we'll see our desperation from a *divine* and *eternal* perspective, we can glimpse God's glory in the midst of all the chaos.

It's in 1 Peter 1:7 (NLT; emphasis mine) that we're told exactly *why* we face these Red Seas of life:

> *"These trials are only to test your faith, to show that it is strong and pure. It is being tested as fire tests and purifies gold—and your faith is far more precious to God than mere gold. So if your faith remains strong after being tried by fiery trials, it will bring you much praise and glory and honor on the day when Jesus Christ is revealed to the whole world."*

God's will is that our faith be *purified* and *strengthened*. Notice the word "fiery" in this Scripture. *Listen*, God has a way of cranking up the furnace to heat levels that make us feel as though we might combust . . . His *will* and *work* are *perfect*, and He's using the fire to remove the dross from our hearts. God knows we have a journey ahead and we'll need to have a pure and solid faith to get us through—life is a seemingly long, yet short, journey, and we'll need faith in Him that can stand the test of time in order to reach our destination. *Within* your faith is God's glory. And believe it or not, you need that *more* than you need your miracle.

You need the assurance of God's presence, power, and peace in *your* life. You need to experience it, and you need to know that God is all knowing *and* all loving. You need to know His grace abounds when life tries to close in on you—your Red Sea moment is preparing you for that miracle. Faith is the bridge that allows your faith to grow exceedingly and allows the promises of God that are known by you to be fully grasped. In times of desperation, God takes your faith and *preserves* and *perfects* it under its trial. *God knows what He's doing*—even if it doesn't seem like He does.

God's will continually seems unreasonable. God doesn't require us to understand His will, just to walk in it. And most of the time, God's will isn't going to make much sense: God told

Noah to build an ark 120 years before a drop of rain ever fell (Genesis 5). David only had a slingshot and a stone to defeat a giant—God doesn't need an army to accomplish His purposes (1 Samuel 17). Jesus told the fishermen who would become His disciples to cast their nets in the middle of the day instead of the middle of the night, when fish were usually caught (John 21), and Jesus didn't hurry to His close friend's bedside to prevent him from passing and everyone from mourning—He waited and raised him from the dead (John 11).

God's will *always* has eternity in mind—our will barely takes us into the next few minutes. We want *out*, we want to be rescued, delivered—we want the *"joys to come that will last forever"* to come *now* ... and we demand *a miracle*. We can't see past our *troubles*; we're convinced that *they* will last forever.

> *"So we don't look at the troubles we can see right now; rather, we look forward to what we have not yet seen. For the troubles we see will soon be over, but **the joys to come will last forever**."* (2 Corinthians 4:18 NLT; emphasis mine)

If you're walking with God, you need to know three things about faith:

1. Your faith will be tested. So, as much as we'd like to skip out on this part of faith, there's no way around it. The very nature of faith demands that it be tested. You can *say* you believe in the promises of God, but if you never have the opportunity to exercise that faith, *your faith is never proven*. *God knows* your measure of faith, *but do you*? How can you be fully ready for the trials that life brings if you're led by your fears instead of being confident in faith? You need to know where you stand in your faith at all times. Because at some point, you'll face a Red Sea or two, or three, or many more than you ever anticipated.

You'll need to *be ready* to trust God, so that you're not consumed by your circumstances. And *every* test you face in life strengthens your faith. If you'll dare to trust God, you'll find yourself believing the promises, holding onto their assurances, *even while their fulfillment is delayed*. Faith *expects* the *unexpected*, especially from a God who *specializes* in miracles.

When you continue to expect the promise you've prayed upon and move forward in faith, taking the very next step God puts in front of you, until the miracle happens, *your faith is perfected*—it's then that your faith becomes more precious than gold. Your test of faith is teaching you to grab hold of the promises of God, pleading them before His throne of grace, and expecting Him to take action upon them. Stand in faith with expectation—*expectation for God to act* without the expectations of *how* and *when* He'll do it—leave the *details* to God. *Only He knows* your life from beginning to end, and His ways are *perfect*.

"God's way is perfect. All the LORD's promises prove true."
(2 Samuel 22:31 NLT)

And here's the truth: *great tests of faith* bring about *great faith*. If you're going through extreme testing, know that God is growing your faith in proportion to it. Tests of life are the element of faith because *untried faith is no faith at all*. If your faith can't stand the test, what good is it? Your faith is being tested to *prove* its strength. And it's not to prove it to God—He's testing it and proving it for your benefit, *not His*.

2. Your faith will be tested in unique and personal ways.
God is all about getting one-on-one with you. You can be a spectator of faith all your life, but God wants you in the game. He wants you to experience a miracle that is so personal and intricate that you'll know it was uniquely designed just for you. He

wants you to know He is God, the great I AM, the one who is the same yesterday, today, and forever (Hebrews 13:8). And when He shows up, He wants you certain that it was Him, not just a coincidence.

"Coincidence is God's way of remaining anonymous."
—Albert Einstein, *The World as I See It*

If you're looking for a miracle, and you're walking in faith, you're going to need to draw near to Him, and that means getting *one-on-one*. A personal relationship with you is what God is after . . . and that may entail *conviction* by His *consuming* fire (Deuteronomy 4:24). As you cry out to God in the midst of your trial, don't miss out on the prayer that changes everything and leads you into the miracle you're seeking:

"Search me, O God, and know my heart; test me and know my anxious thoughts. Point out anything in me that offends you, and lead me along the path of everlasting life." (Psalm 139:23–24 NLT)

KNOW THIS: WHEN YOU PRAY THIS PRAYER OF ACTIVE FAITH, *you may not like the answer.* Fellowship with God is essential to faith, and fellowship with God means allowing Him to consume, correct, and convict us . . . *while He comforts us.* And know that His grace will be enough when He dissects your heart and reveals the sin within it—His grace is ALWAYS amazing. Allow Him to work within you as He works in and through your circumstances to purge all that keeps you from being in a perfect relationship with Him.

3. God will use your pain and suffering for purposes that are greater than you can imagine. You can't see it now, but God can *and does.* What you're suffering through right now, the fear that overwhelms you and the pain that consumes you, God will bring about purpose from it. You can count on it. God wastes nothing ... *nothing*. So don't for a second believe that your situation is an exception. Though we'd like the sufferings of our lives to be used for purposes that lift up *ourselves*, it's all about us becoming *less* and God becoming *more* (John 3:30). *It's not about you*, and that's a hard pill to swallow. If you can view your pain and suffering, your test of faith, as a benefit for the kingdom of God, you'll find God's grace alleviating the emptiness that has left you hopeless. Although difficult to grasp, your trial may simply be for *someone else's good, not your own*. Jesus put it this way:

> *"Love each other in the same way I have loved you. There is no greater love than to lay down one's life for one's friends. You are my friends if you do what I command. I no longer call you slaves, because a master doesn't confide in his slaves. Now you are my friends, since I have told you everything the Father told me. You didn't choose me. I chose you. I appointed you to go and produce lasting fruit, so that the Father will give you whatever you ask for, using my name. This is my command: Love each other."* (John 15:12–17 NLT)

Listen, trials of life truly feel as though you're "*laying your life down*." And you might not realize it now, but you may very well be laying your life down without realizing it. That boss who continually harasses you, to whom you respond in kindness, may one day find his heart altered by God, leading to salvation. Those children you're sacrificing for, enduring a painful marriage so that you can protect and nurture them in the ways of the Lord, may change the world through their own faith as a result of your own. The cancer that is eating away at your body and soul may be the perfect setup for a miracle that will yield your victory as a trophy of hope and encouragement for someone else suffering through the same situation. Let God work in your life *and* through your pain—though He *contests* your faith, be assured, He's only *confirming* it.

> *"The way to stronger faith usually lies along the rough pathway of sorrow. Only as faith is contested, will faith be confirmed."*
> —C. H. Spurgeon

The hard-to-grasp truth is that, when all is said and done, when the Red Sea has been parted, the waves have taken down the enemy, and the promised land lies ahead of us, we will find the good that we receive through our pain and sorrows *incalculable.*

God's grace will come from places in your life you never expected. And when you're searching to make some kind of sense of all that you're going through, know that in your days without trial, you'll seldom discover greater faith—*faith comes when you need it.* When everything in your life is stripped bare and you're empty, without hope, *your faith is revealed.* And sometimes, that's all your trial may be about: *revealing the state of your faith.*

> *"Birds' nests are hard to find in summertime, but anyone can find a bird's nest in winter. When all the leaves are off the trees, the nests are visible to all."* —Reverend William Jay

We can find ourselves declaring, as David did in Psalm 119:71–72 (NLT; emphasis mine):

> *"My suffering was good for me, for it taught me to pay attention to your decrees. Your instructions are more valuable to me than millions in gold and silver."*

Unfortunately for us, sometimes suffering is the only thing that gets our attention and draws us nearer to God. So, in this light, we can actually see our suffering, our Red Sea moment of consuming fear, as God's *mercy.* It's actually the severity of our trials that enables us to experience more divine grace and unthinkable glory; though, at the time, it will hardly seem like God's mercy, but more like His *wrath*. You won't see purpose in it, *but God* will, and if you'll trust Him completely, His miracles will be beyond all that you can imagine.

Faith isn't easy, but it makes all things possible—*all things.* Yet it's only in the will of God that we experience the miracles, and we need to be certain we're in His will. Being in His will is all about walking by faith, and walking by faith can only happen one way—*by trusting in His Word.* It's His promises that pave the path to His greatest miracles. So cling tightly to His promises and *faith will come.*

> *"So faith comes from hearing the message, and the message that is heard is what Christ spoke."* (Romans 10:17 GOD'S WORD)

We need to be certain of a few things about faith. Faith is not derived from emotions. Emotions don't believe, *they feel.* Emotions react, *faith never does.* The determining factor of the state of your faith will be your relationship with God. Because without trusting God, *you'll lack faith.* In those moments, when you're seeking which direction to take, you'll need to not demand that God work things out your way; you'll need to fully surrender to His. There's *no other way* to walk on dry land through a parted Red Sea. If God has prepared the way, He'll make it clear, and the miracles will fall in place. Don't force God's hand, *just hold tight to it.* God has a will and a purpose for you—you'll just need to accept His invitation into His will, *instead of continually trying to invite Him into your own.*

Listen, God knows you need a miracle ... *truly He does.* And He also knows that only He can do the impossible. He's not holding out on you, He's not playing games—He's working *within* you in *unseen* ways that will yield *unthinkable* glory. But in those moments of despair, *you'll lack faith,* and you'll wonder what He's up to. You'll find yourself unable to really pray, mostly filled with bitterness and resentment over the injustices in your life. And you'll have to surrender to God's will, asking God to do whatever it takes to build the necessary faith in you.

Our part in our Red Sea moments is to *surrender* and *seek* God with all that we are—trusting Him to catch us up in His purposes—knowing that you won't see or understand His purposes in the moment. If you're walking by faith, *you won't have the sight to see what God is doing.* He works in seen *and* unseen ways—mostly unseen, and that can be discouraging because that's not how we hoped faith worked.

Too often, we won't know the *specific* will of God, but we know He has a will, and so the only thing we'll be able to do is to seek Him. We'll need to let go of our desire to be God and realize that *we can't use faith as a force of our own.* We can't manipulate our emotions, trying to feel as if we believe, yet finding ourselves overwhelmed and panicked over the fact that we don't feel as if we have faith. Faith is trusting in God's word, believing what He's promised, and surrendering to Him fully. Though we're exhausted from the age-old saying, we must truly *"Let go and let God."*

Every miracle of God comes with one prerequisite—faith. *And faith surrenders.* Faith is the evidence in you that you've fully surrendered, yielded to God, and are completely trusting Him with the outcome. If we'll yield to God, there's no way we'll miss His will, and if we're in His will, *miracles are sure to happen.* We must submit to God in faith and submit to Him *for* it.

Fully trust that God has a plan to bring about good from your pain and suffering. Rest under the shadow of His wings

(Psalm 17:8), know that God isn't making things up as He goes along ... He's not expecting you to figure it all out; He's not asking you to create your own faith to summon a miracle out of heaven; He's already working the miracle ... *He just wants you to trust Him.*

Yet, we can trust, and find ourselves puzzled by the pieces that just aren't fitting together. It's in understanding the *ways* of God that we can grow to know the *will* of God, and when God is leading us into His will, He does it two ways:

1. God leads us by His word. We can't live without the word of God ... we can, but we won't be in His will and we won't find ourselves witnessing miracles. Jesus said:

"People do not live by bread alone, but by every word that comes from the mouth of God." (Matthew 4:4 NLT)

We shouldn't try and move ahead of God; it *never* ends up well. God has specific and individual plans for each of us, and we can look at Saul's life in order to better understand how God will lead, guide, and direct us.

It was in Saul's everyday, mundane life that he was called to something extraordinary (1 Samuel 9:1–7). God has a habit of stepping into people's lives and setting them on a path of divine design. God loves to use unlikely characters to change the course of history, and that takes miracles, which is why we need to be aware that our Red Sea moment may be the very trial that presents God's will for our life.

God's plans for us, His direction for our lives, won't always seem clear. *That's on purpose.* God wants us relying on Him every moment of every day, every step of the way. In verse 5 of 1 Samuel 9, we find Saul discouraged and ready to give up—it was a servant who suggested that they ask for God's direction before quitting. Exhaustion from life can cause you to act outside of God's will—realize that problems and pressures will do that. And when you walk outside of God's will and begin relying on your own resources, working in your own strength, *you'll become discouraged.* In moments like these, you'll need to run to God for help because *He* is your strength and portion.

> *"My flesh and my heart may fail, but God is the strength of my heart and my portion forever."* (Psalm 73:26 NIV)

Know that if you're walking with God, walking in faith, even when you're not sure just how much you have, God will move ahead of you and prepare the way. *God had a vision of parting the Red Sea, long before He parted it.* "God knew." And in 1 Samuel 9:15, we find that before Saul met the prophet Samuel, God had spoken to Samuel, revealing His plan for Saul.

God is working out your miracle, even when you're not aware of it. Sometimes there are divine puzzle pieces that simply aren't ready to be put together yet. Have you ever learned the steps of putting together a puzzle? Step one tells us that the border of the puzzle should be put together first because they all have straight edges and they are easier to put together. God can often work in the same way when it comes to our lives. He'll establish the framework and then begin working on the pieces that fill up the rest of our lives. But it happens piece by piece.

Your life will come together the same way—through your faith—piece by piece. Each piece interlocks with the next in a precise and particular way according to God's plans for you. And it's our faith in His word that creates the border, the framework of our lives. Our only responsibility is to walk by faith and trust God to put the pieces of our life together, until its completion.

Know that as you trust God to work out the details of your life in accordance to His will, He will always start with a vision that He'll plant in your heart and mind. He'll plant a seed and then grow it with His grace. And know that God's plans for your life will always go beyond *your* abilities and resources—He wants you relying on Him at all times. You'll get a vision from God and realize that you're *unworthy* and *unable*, and *you are*. It's His grace that will enable you to do all that He wants you to do.

Once the vision is given, God will walk you through paths that lead you into His presence, so that He can build a relationship with you, in order to give you the wisdom and guidance you'll need with each step you take.

As God leads you in His will, you'll find your circumstances taking on new meaning—things that used to have little to no significance will suddenly be *vitally* important. Your eyes will be opened to every detail of life around you and you'll be suddenly aware that God is doing things in supernatural ways on extraordinarily mundane days.

And know that there will be opposition to what God's called you to do. As you walk faithfully into God's will for your life, there will be a wall of darkness that will close in on you from time to time. There will be people who will ridicule your life's transformation, there will be those who will be skeptical about God's call on your life and the direction you're taking, and you'll begin to doubt you're walking in God's will at all ... *but keep your eyes on God*. He's all you need when the feelings of inadequacy and unworthiness overwhelm you. Above all else, keep taking a step of faith and trusting God—no one has been called to live your life but you. God has specifically designed you for your journey—trust that He knows what He's doing.

When your faith is focused, you'll find that there is great peace in walking in His will, but go ahead of him and all hell will break loose. We find, in 1 Samuel 23:7, that when Saul heard that David was trapped in a walled town, he assumed that God was working mightily and putting David at His mercy. Saul's selfish motives got in the way of God's plan and caused him to move ahead of God's will. We must continually stay connected to God and His word or we'll misinterpret *our* will for *God's*.

We should only seek the direction God's given us, and He's given us direction through His word. We can be absolutely certain that God will never lead us in a way that is contrary to what He says in the Bible. We can count on God to keep His word and we can find strength and comfort by being led by it. Faith in God's word will keep us right in the center of His will.

2. God leads us by His peace. Too often, we get frustrated because we can't seem to find God specifically speaking about our circumstances in His word. We struggle with hearing Him, and we can find ourselves paving our own paths *when we can't seem to find clarity in His promises.* The peace of God can't be counterfeited; His presence and peace will sometimes be all you have in the darkest night to get you through. When you've lost all perspective because life has taken some detours that have led to destructive dead ends, God's peace will be the saving grace that enables you to seek Him in faith. Seek God and seek His peace, and *don't stop* seeking. It's when you fully trust God that you'll find His peace ... and it's only then that you can *"lean not unto your own understanding,"* so that He can direct your path.

> *"Trust in the LORD with all your heart; do not depend on your own understanding. Seek his will in all you do, and he will show you which path to take."* (Proverbs 3:5–6 NLT)

Listen, it's easier said than done, so don't lose faith just because you're consumed with *"leaning on your own understanding."* We struggle with our faith because we're continually looking for outward signs that God is working on a miracle in our life. *We forget that God moves in an unseen realm.* As we desperately seek God's will, we will need to turn our heart to God's. When you don't know what God's will is, you can do two things that will align your spirit with His:

1. Obey what God has commanded you to do. Sometimes God's commands are obvious—He's given us the Bible as our instruction book for life. Yet sometimes His will for our lives is not so clearly laid out. It's difficult, at best, to obey God in greater things that require more discernment than it is to obey the more direct and simple commands like "do not lie, cheat, or steal." We'll struggle with the next steps in faith if we aren't in line with God's specific and direct will.

Once we're obeying diligently in the small things, God leads us on to greater things. *Leaving Egypt was easy.* The Israelites had waited endlessly for God to make a way for their escape, but *the Red Sea challenged their faith in ways they wished it hadn't.* And God will test our faith in new ways along our journey of life, bringing us to our knees more often than we'd like. He's developing our character and perfecting our spirit, paving our path into eternity.

If we'll be faithful in what God has asked of us in His *specific* will, we can be sure that He will reveal more and more of Himself and His overall will, which takes us into the unseen realm ... *that's where faith takes us.*

2. Pray and seek God's wisdom and guidance at all times. A hard truth to accept is that a Christian is no greater than his prayer life. The first thing we should do tends to be the last action we take—*pray*. We like to make our plans and then ask God to bless them. We think we've got life figured out, until we find ourselves in desperation and realize *we don't*.

The nation of Israel learned the hard way that they needed God's constant guidance, in Joshua 9:1–18. Israel had just entered the promised land and found themselves basking in the victory that came from enjoying God's blessings. And they found great comfort and strength in knowing that God had promised they would have victory, as long as they remained obedient. But Joshua, just like us, became careless and overconfident.

You see, God had instructed Israel to destroy every nation within a specific set of boundaries. The other nations were concerned and afraid of being destroyed, so the people of Gibeon created a plan to manipulate and deceive Israel into making a peace treaty with them. The plan was to make Israel think that they were *not* one of the targeted nations. Israel acted in haste and days later discovered they had been deceived. *It was too late.* Because of the peace treaty, that nation was a continual problem for Israel and we learn that the reason for such a tragic turn in God's plan for Israel was because the word of the Lord was not kept, a medium was consulted for guidance, and they "*did not inquire of the Lord*" (1 Chronicles 10:14 NIV).

Tragic events throughout history have centered around people making decisions without consulting God—*making their own plans instead of seeking His*. Don't make the same mistake that so many have. Seek God *in* everything, *for* everything, and above all else, never take another step until you're certain that God has made His will clear to you. You won't want to wait, *but you'll have to*. God rarely gives a "drive-through" answer. More than likely He is going to use the situation to draw you nearer to Him so that He can develop a deeper relationship with you and strengthen your faith. So don't rush the process—you'll miss out on God's greatest work in your life. Just keep seeking Him, and His grace will be there when you need it.

So the *second secret* of faith is to draw near to God, pray for His will, and trust that He has plans and purposes that go far beyond your own. Here's the truth, when you're doubting a miracle will ever come: *God is able.* The question is, "Do *you* believe He is?"

> *Passive faith accepts the word as true*
> *But never moves.*
> *Active faith begins the work to do,*
> *And thereby proves.*
> *Passive faith says,*
> *"I believe it! Every word of God is true.*
> *Well I know He hath not spoken what He cannot,*
> *will not, do.*
> *He hath bidden me, 'Go forward!'*
> *but a closed-up way I see,*
> *When the waters are divided,*
> *soon in Canaan's land I'll be.*
> *Lo! I hear His voice commanding,*
> *'Rise and walk: take up thy bed';*
> *And, 'Stretch forth thy withered member!'*
> *which for so long has been dead.*
> *When I am a little stronger then,*
> *I know I'll surely stand:*
> *When there comes a thrill of healing,*
> *I will use with ease my other hand.*
> *Yes, I know that 'God is able' and full willing all to do:*
> *I believe that every promise, sometime,*
> *will to me come true."*

Active faith says, "I believe it!
And the promise now I take,
Knowing well, as I receive it,
God, each promise, real will make.
So I step into the waters, finding there an open way;
Onward press, the land possessing;
nothing can my progress stay.
Yea, I rise at His commanding,
walk straightway, and joyfully:
This, my hand, so sadly shriveled, as I reach,
restored shall be.
What beyond His faithful promise,
would I wish or do I need?
Looking not for 'signs or wonders,'
I'll no contradiction heed.
Well I know that 'God is able,'
and full willing all to do:
I believe that every promise,
at this moment can come true."
Passive faith but praises in the light,
When sun doth shine.
Active faith will praise in darkest night—
Which faith is thine?

—L. B. Cowman, *Streams in the Desert*

3

KEEP YOUR EYES
ON GOD

Faith is all about focus. Determining where your focus is will give a good indication as to the state of your faith. When Moses was chosen to lead God's people out of slavery, it was only *one* thing that kept him moving in the right direction—*he kept focused on God*—but his focus lost its way from time to time, *just like ours does*. Moses had questions that demanded answers, but he often got none. When our circumstances contain overwhelming pain and suffering, along with despair and uncertainty, our vision becomes blurred.

As Moses struggled to follow God's directions and obey His every command, we find that Moses's path to the miracles first came by way of a refusal. Moses didn't want to follow God's plan, and when God asks us to step out in faith, most of the time we don't want to walk in His will either. It often requires us to walk through uncertainty that brings us to our knees—but that's right where God wants us, because we have nowhere to look but *up*. And when we're looking up, our eyes and heart will be focused on God, the God who is working the miracles.

Moses's journey of faith began with a burning bush. It was his one on one with God. Sometimes God will speak to us in a burning-bush moment, and sometimes He will speak to us in a still, small voice.

> *"And behold, the Lord passed by, and a great and strong wind rent the mountains and broke in pieces the rocks before the Lord, but the Lord was not in the wind; and after the wind an earthquake, but the Lord was not in the earthquake; And after the earthquake a fire, but the Lord was not in the fire; and after the fire [a sound of gentle stillness and] a still, small voice."* (1 Kings 19:11–12 AMP)

Sometimes God speaks to us in His still, small voice; at other times it's in earthshaking, breathtaking ways. Just draw near to Him and allow Him to show up in the way He sees fit to have the greatest impact on your faith. And then don't make excuses like Moses did. Because here's the thing: the beginnings of the Red Sea miracle began with fear, and your miracles will begin that way too. It's not that easy to say, "Yes, Lord, Your will be done." We mostly pray, "thy will be done," yet demand our own.

Moses, who led the Israelites to their Red Sea miracle, doubted God, and so do we. His story gives us the ability to take a more realistic look at our own. And that should give us hope and faith in realizing that God sees past our fears and into our hearts. He sees the faith in us that we can't and He carefully leads us step by step into the miracles He has already planned for us.

In Exodus 3:7–10 we find God revealing His plan to Moses, only to have Moses reply with a list of excuses that we've more than likely versed to God ourselves.

We tend to believe that we're not worthy, unable and unequipped for what God is leading us through, what He's called us to do in faith. And we're right: we're not able to bring about the miracles in our lives, only God can. So, in verse 11, Moses's excuse, "*Who am I, that I should go to Pharaoh and bring the Israelites out of Egypt?*" was a simple response of fear, not unlike the fear we experience when God is leading us to places in our faith that we're not sure we want to go. But God's response to Moses is no different than His response to us when He's called us to step out in faith and beyond our fears: "*I will be with you*" (verse 12). Believe this truth as you struggle to let go of a past you so desperately need to let go of, but can't seem to find the courage to move forward in faith. God promises His presence and gives us the assurance that "all things work together for good." But when we're consumed with fear, we don't always see it that way, and neither did Moses.

Moses's next question mimics our own—we want to know whose authority are we acting upon. When we're facing ridicule and we begin to doubt the faith we're walking in, we want to know whom it is we're putting our trust in. So Moses asks the question we'd like to know as well:

> "*Suppose I go to the Israelites and say to them, 'The God of your fathers has sent me to you,' and they ask me, 'What is his name?' Then what shall I tell them?'*" (verse 13)

As usual, God answers Moses as directly as He answers us through His word: "*I am who I am*" (verse 14). And that's all we need to know. *God is God and we are not.*

Moses works past his first two excuses and leads into the third: "*What if they do not believe me or listen to me?*" (Exodus 4:1). Maybe Moses didn't quite hear God right earlier in the conversation—doubt and fear was getting the best of him, and it gets the best of us too. God had assured Moses that the people would listen to him, but Moses didn't take God at His word.

We, just like Moses, doubt God's sovereignty; so God begins to work miracles through Moses (turning a staff into a snake and turning water into blood). God knew exactly how to strengthen Moses's faith and He knows how to strengthen yours. You'll find that when there's a setup to a big miracle in your life, there are little ones that lead the way. For some reason, we see fit to demand miracles along our faith journey ... we have a difficult time taking God at His word.

> *"Unless you see signs or wonders, you will never believe."* (John 4:48 NIV)

We fail to recognize, as we're praying for a miracle, that God wants us to play a role in the miracles in our lives. He wants us to fully experience His *hand* as we surrender our *heart*. As Moses struggles to understand this truth, he makes another excuse to try and thwart God's will: "*O Lord, I have never been eloquent, neither in the past nor since you have spoken to your servant. I am slow of speech and tongue*" (verse 10). We wonder, "What does it take for Moses to trust God?" What will it take for us to trust Him? At first glance we'd believe that Moses's reluctance to obey God is due to his humble admission of his lack of abilities, yet it only reveals his lack of trust in God's. If we'd simply take God at His word, we'd see His faithfulness and refuse to ever doubt again.

Your confidence in God's will isn't going to come from yourself or others. It won't come from how your circumstances are shaping up. It's going to come from listening to God, what He's spoken through His word, and realizing that God has equipped us and will enable us to walk in the path He's prepared for us. God loves doing the impossible and He loves using people who feel as though they are limited in resources or inadequate. It's in those hearts that God's glory is most easily recognized. God tells us in 2 Corinthians 12:9, "*My grace is sufficient for you, for my power is made perfect in weakness."* His grace is all we need. God's greatest work is done when we're weakest and His greatest miracles are done through Red Sea moments.

We find ourselves desperately wanting to trust God, but looking at the raging Red Sea before us and the army ready to attack, we want *out.* We ask God to make another way than the one He's taking us. In verse 13 we find Moses asking, *"O Lord, please send someone else to do it."* But if we refuse to trust God, we walk away from miracles. Deep down we want to trust God, but feelings get in the way and fear gets the best of us. It's when we're willing to step out in faith and obey Him that we'll experience the miracles we pray for.

If we'll trust God and His will for us, we'll find ourselves witnessing unquestionable evidence of His power and presence in our lives like never before.

But know that even when you decide to trust God, accepting His will and readily walking in it, your faith will be tested; you will find yourself not only being led to do what is *right,* but learning to discern what is *wrong,* and your faith will have to have the focus to refuse what is wrong. You'll need to turn your eyes from what hinders your relationship with God and keep your mind focused upon Him so that you'll have peace amid the fear and uncertainty, as you wait on Him to work your miracle. God promises that if we keep focused upon Him, He'll give us His perfect peace.

"You will keep in perfect peace those whose minds are stead-fast, because they trust in you." (Isaiah 26:3 NIV)

When your faith is tested and you find yourself stumped by the questions that life is throwing at you, you'll need to take EVERY thought captive. Though the battle seems to be amid your circumstances, it takes place in an unseen world. The battle will rage within your spirit, in the recesses of your mind. Your greatest weapon in the fight of faith will be 2 Corinthians 10:5:

> *"We destroy every proud obstacle that keeps people from knowing God. We capture their rebellious thoughts and teach them to obey Christ."* (NLT)

More often than not, we're taking direction from our emotions and thoughts. They become obstacles to our miracles and it's in taking every thought captive that our faith and the spirit of God work together. When our faith acts upon the promises of God, we are no longer at the mercy of our thoughts, doubts, and fears. When we teach our thoughts to obey Christ, fear and faith collide and the result is hope for the miracle you're seeking.

It's in Red Sea moments where you'll find yourself at the point where you've lost all hope and you believe the miracle is not going to come. You'll find yourself filled with despair and uncertain if you can make it through the next moment, much less through the day, so you'll need to focus upon God … not because you feel like it, but because that's what faith does. You'll need to focus upon God's goodness in your past, His presence in the present moment, and His power to handle whatever lies ahead in the future. And you'll find yourself at more than one Red Sea moment in life … *you'll face many.* And each time you stand facing the raging waters ready to take you *under* and the army ready to take you *out,* you'll need to look *up,* when everything's got you *down.*

> *"When I had lost all hope, I turned my thoughts once more to the Lord."* (Jonah 2:7 LB)

At times, you *will* lose hope, because you *will* walk by sight. It happens to all those who dare to trust God. If you're ever going to learn to trust God, He knows you're going to have to face the fear that comes from doubting Him. *And He'll make you wait far longer than you'd like.* He'll allow you to face insurmountable circumstances and He'll make you wait, until your faith is perfected. And through the process, He'll teach you how to trust Him, even when there's no evidence that you should.

Staying focused upon God won't come easy, but you can do three things that will help you keep your faith focused while you wait upon your miracle:

1. Don't look back. It's been said, *"If you're not moving forward, you're moving backward."* God doesn't want us focused on the past ... *there's no past in our future.* We, just like the Israelites, start second-guessing God in our Red Sea moments. We struggle to look ahead because all we know is our present pain, and we begin to wonder if the past was that bad after all. The Israelites were slaves, longing to be free, praying day and night that God would break the chains that bound them. And then when He did, and He led them into a fearful place, they questioned His entire plan and doubted His loving hand.

> *"As Pharaoh approached, the Israelites looked up, and there were the Egyptians, marching after them. They were terrified and cried out to the LORD. They said to Moses, 'Was it because there were no graves in Egypt that you brought us to the desert to die? What have you done to us by bringing us out of Egypt? Didn't we say to you in Egypt, "Leave us alone; let us serve the Egyptians"? It would have been better for us to serve the Egyptians than to die in the desert!'"* (Exodus 14:10–12 NIV)

It's healthy to look back at the past and reflect upon where we went wrong, where we went right, and on the grace of God in our lives through it all—but it's not OK to *dwell* there. The true purpose of looking back is to remind us of God's faithfulness—

His grace that found us and poured down upon us when we least expected it and clearly didn't deserve it. We can spend so much time in the past and second guessing God that we'll lose focus . . . and our faith will fail. Reflect upon God's faithfulness; though He may have led you *in*, He'll give you strength through His promises as you trust Him to lead you *out*.

2. Stay focused on where you are. You'll never be able to change the past, but you can completely affect your future. If we reflect on our past, we need to make sure that time is put to good use by applying what we've learned about our faith in the past and using those lessons to impact our future in a way that brings glory to God. Whatever situation we're in, whatever overwhelming circumstances we're facing, we need to realize that all is *not* lost. If we realize we're right where God wants us, we can find the strength we need to take one more step of faith in the present moment. Although it may not seem like God has a plan to give us a future and a hope, He's promised that He does, and if we'll stay focused in the here and now, we'll realize that what we view as *the end*, in the hands of God, is only the *beginning*.

3. Trust that God is good. This won't be easy, because even if you believe God is good, life says something entirely different. There will be many, many times in your life when you will truly doubt that God is good—when you find yourself married to an addict; when you hear the word "cancer"; when you're left jobless, homeless, and hopeless; when taking your own life seems like the best option. You'll be fully convinced that God is anything *but* good. You'll have to make the decision to trust God and *you won't want to*. And you will struggle in the fact that you know that miracles only come by trusting in God, but you don't feel like you have the faith to trust Him into the very next hour. And your only choice will be to trust God because in Red Sea moments, it's all you can do. You'll find that the only thing that will get you through and keep you walking in faith is keeping your eyes on God and your heart clinging to His promises. And you'll need to trust Him when He says His grace is sufficient—it *always has been* and *always will be* (Hebrews 13:8).

Know this: no matter how hard you try, you'll lose focus from time to time. The Israelites on their journey through Exodus certainly did, and you will too ... so don't get too down on yourself. Life's circumstances can distract us. And though the things that distract us from God may not in and of themselves be bad in their nature, they can become our greatest obstacles if they stand in the way of God's will for our lives. We can't be ignorant of those things that will trip us up and distract us from keeping our eyes focused on God.

> *"Since we are surrounded by so many examples of faith, we must get rid of everything that slows us down, especially sin that distracts us. We must run the race that lies ahead of us and never give up."* (Hebrews 12:1 GOD'S WORD)

The most common things that distract us from God are sometimes obvious, but at other times not:

1. Money. Maybe this one seems obvious, but seldom do we recognize that money is distracting us from God until it's too late. We're to *live* in this world, *but not be of it*, or *owned by it*. Money is not in itself an obstacle to our walk with God, but our love of money is. When we're more focused on what money provides instead of God's provision, we'll find ourselves struggling in our walk of faith. You've read these words many times before, but take a moment in your desperation, when you're facing your Red Sea, and hear the gentle yet assuring voice of God Almighty saying, *"Trust Me, I am with you, and I am everything you need."*

"Don't store up treasures here on earth, where moths eat them and rust destroys them, and where thieves break in and steal. Store your treasures in heaven, where moths and rust cannot destroy, and thieves do not break in and steal. Wherever your treasure is, there the desires of your heart will also be.

"Your eye is a lamp that provides light for your body. When your eye is good, your whole body is filled with light. But when your eye is bad, your whole body is filled with darkness. And if the light you think you have is actually darkness, how deep that darkness is!

"No one can serve two masters. For you will hate one and love the other; you will be devoted to one and despise the other. You cannot serve both God and money.

"That is why I tell you not to worry about everyday life—whether you have enough food and drink, or enough clothes to wear. Isn't life more than food, and your body more than clothing? Look at the birds. They don't plant or harvest or store food in barns, for your heavenly Father feeds them. And aren't you far more valuable to him than they are? Can all your worries add a single moment to your life?

"And why worry about your clothing? Look at the lilies of the field and how they grow. They don't work or make their clothing, yet Solomon in all his glory was not dressed as beautifully as they are. And if God cares so wonderfully for wildflowers that are here today and thrown into the fire tomorrow, he will certainly care for you. Why do you have so little faith?

"So don't worry about these things, saying, 'What will we eat? What will we drink? What will we wear?' These things dominate the thoughts of unbelievers, but your heavenly Father already knows all your needs. Seek the Kingdom of God above all else, and live righteously, and he will give you everything you need.

"So don't worry about tomorrow, for tomorrow will bring its own worries. Today's trouble is enough for today."
(Matthew 6:19–34, NLT)

If Jesus himself were before you at this moment, looking into your eyes and speaking these words, would you view your situation any differently? If you were certain that God would provide your every need, why would there be any need to worry? But the Israelites did. And instead of God pouring down manna from heaven, He asked them to trust Him *every single* day. He provided ONLY what they needed for each day and they were forced to continually come to His throne of grace. He's doing the same in your life.

> *"Then the LORD said to Moses, 'I will rain down bread from heaven for you. The people are to go out each day and gather enough for that day. In this way I will test them and see whether they will follow my instructions.'"* (Exodus 16:4 NIV)

Once again we're reminded that God is continually testing and proving our faith. Not for His benefit, but for ours. He's always teaching us to trust Him and pressing us into impossible places to prove His faithfulness. The question will always be, will you trust Him and will you obey Him, *even in your doubt*?

2. Media. Whether we'd like to admit it or not, this distraction is ever increasing to such a degree that we're desensitized to the fact that it's actually keeping us from our relationship with God. We are bombarded with influences that tell us how to live, tell us what's important, and define what's right and wrong. We so easily set the Bible aside for entertainment that adds little to no value to life and can damage our minds in unseen ways. If we're to keep from getting distracted, preventing our faith from giving way to fear, we're going to have to focus our minds.

> *"Fix your thoughts on what is true, and honorable, and right, and pure, and lovely, and admirable. Think about things that are excellent and worthy of praise."* (Philippians 4:8 NLT)

If we're fixing our thoughts, they're unwavering. Our attention gives no way to distractions and we're focused firmly on God, His word, and His will. It means that in every area of life, we're to place God and His instructions for us first and keep ourselves from giving into the ways of this world.

3. Desires. Oddly enough, this is a difficult distraction that we seldom recognize. We want the miracles in our lives more than we want God. We want the gift, not necessarily the giver. It's an easy distraction to fall into. We focus so much on our needs that we easily forget the One who provides them. We daily undergo a constant struggle to keep our eyes focused upon God and not get distracted by the circumstances that cause us to walk by sight instead of by faith.

When we're praying for our miracles in life, we need to remember the vital command in Matthew 6:33:

"Seek the Kingdom of God above all else, and live righteously, and he will give you everything you need."

Everything you need—there's NOTHING that doesn't include.

"Faith expects from God what is beyond all expectation."
—Andrew Murray

So the *third secret* of faith is: keep focused on God at all times and in all things. Never allow anything to stand in the way of your faith—nothing—especially not *fear*.

4

TURN YOUR FEAR
INTO FAITH

Fear has two faces: there's right fear and wrong fear. By definition, we find that fear can either mean a feeling of agitation and
anxiety caused by the presence of imminent danger *or* extreme
reverence or awe, as toward a supreme power. And it's in the
midst of our agitation and anxiety, when we're confused and
uncertain, waiting for a miracle that seems too impossible to
come, that we find that the right fear drives us into extreme
reverence and awe toward God, eliminating the wrong fear, and
leading us through parted waters and upon dry ground.

> *"The remarkable thing about fearing God is that when you*
> *fear God, you fear nothing else, whereas if you do not fear*
> *God, you fear everything else."* —Oswald Chambers

By experience we know that fear works directly against our
faith. Wrong fear will pull us from God and separate us in ways
that cause us to question His presence and His power. In the
process of walking by faith, we learn many things about fear.
And though we'll struggle to reject wrong fear, we can walk in

faith if we understand a few things about fear and faith. First and foremost, we must clearly understand that faith is a *choice*.

We tend to rely on our five senses to guide us through life, and that's where we go *dangerously* and *recklessly* wrong—faith is a choice to believe something and then act upon that belief. It's a choice to believe without assurance, *in the face of doubt*.

When we're faced with a Red Sea moment in life, we find ourselves wondering if we've ever had faith at all. We know it's completely gone at the moment. And though we have trusted God in the past, we often find it difficult to trust Him in our present circumstances. If His grace has been there for us throughout our lives, and we are well aware of it, shouldn't we be beyond faith? The reality of fear keeps us from getting beyond faith, so know this: you will need to walk by faith until you walk into the gates of heaven. So it's vital to understand that you're going to have to continually make a choice to have faith and not rely on your senses before you do.

No matter what our specific situation is, when we find ourselves overwhelmed with fear, faith seems elusive as we work endlessly, sometimes in vain, to reject our fears. Day to day, and hour to hour, we can find fear weakening our faith to such an extent that we become paralyzed, unable to face our problems and find strength to even hold on to what little faith we think we have. So, in order to reject and eliminate our fears, we have to understand their source. We need to understand our *fears* so that we can make way for *faith*.

All too often, life takes us into places of such great despair, accompanied by debilitating worry, that we instinctively begin trying to solve our problems on our own, relying on our own resources. And whether we recognize it or not, even entertaining thoughts of how to solve our own problems creates intense anxiety, in and of itself. Because deep within our souls, we know we are finite and unable to understand the greater picture of our lives. We know, whether we openly admit it or not, we are not God. Yet *we continually try to be.* And that effort leads to a hopelessness we never anticipate amid the crises in our lives. Our fear comes from the reality of knowing that we are not capable of changing ourselves or our circumstances. And when we aren't in control, we feel confident that life can't possibly be either.

But faith says something different. Faith can only overcome our fears when we rely on our memories of God's previous work in our lives, and His promises throughout history regarding the past, present, and future. Yet life can take some unexpected turns and our faith can become vulnerable when our present circumstances contradict what we believe to be true.

Our fears arise when we're painfully aware that we have no idea what today will hold, no clue about tomorrow, and although we may believe in God's love for us, it's the seemingly impossible challenges in our lives that dominate our thoughts and cause us to doubt whether God is hearing our prayers at all. In the face of our fear, we have to choose to move forward on the basis of faith, not feelings. *And sometimes we have to do it afraid.* And we have to choose faith for as long as it takes because it's our choice of faith that will sooner or later give way to miracles.

Don't be surprised by your fears; just choose faith for the moment so that God can work. Fear will send the walls of water caving in—*faith parts them.* And here's the thing to remember: *things aren't always as bad as you think they are.* Although everything within you will be convinced that things are much worse, allow your fear to drive you to God. He moves powerfully within humble hearts that surrender at His throne of grace.

We can allow the wrong fear to bring us into right fear, because fear should alarm us to the fact that we've distanced ourselves from God and we need to draw near to Him and have our faith restored. In our weakness, *He will be your strength.*

We must always take our fear to the Lord. We must continually humble our hearts and realize that when we're overcome with fear, we've forgotten God's *power* and His *plans.* It's out of fear that we tend to pray, *"my will,"* instead of *"thy will,"* and that's where we get into trouble.

If we're humble, we'll be working constantly to choose attitudes and actions that will strengthen our faith, *eliminating our fears.* When we're trusting in God's promises, approaching His throne of grace with an open heart, we find that it's through our humility that we *choose* faith.

Our fear is merely a prompting to return to God, who has never left our side. And it's through our returning to Him that He blesses us with hope for the miracle we need.

Don't be deceived, *fear is a part of having faith.* You will experience fear—it's not a matter of *if*, but *when*—but what you do with fear is entirely up to you.

> *"When I am afraid, I put my trust in you. In God, whose word I praise—in God I trust and am not afraid."* (Psalm 56:3–4 NIV)

So we need to learn to let go of our fears and give God control. We need steps in overcoming our fears with faith, by taking practical steps in humility—acknowledging that we are afraid and in desperate need for God's presence, power, and peace:

1. Be assured of God's love for you. You need to clearly understand that *"God so loved the world"* (John 3:16) and YOU are in this world. You may not feel as though God loves you, but He's promised that He does, no matter who you are or what you've done. He's forgiven you, past, present, and future, when you seek the savior he sent to save you—His love for you is boundless.

"We are made right in God's sight when we trust in Jesus Christ to take away our sins. And we all can be saved in this same way, no matter who we are or what we have done." (Romans 3:22 NLT)

You will never be able to fully grasp God's love for you, but it's vital that you *accept* His love, even if you can't understand it.

"When I think of the wisdom and the scope of God's plan, I fall to my knees and pray to the Father, the Creator of everything in heaven and on earth. I pray that from his glorious, unlimited resources he will give you mighty inner strength through his Holy Spirit. And I pray that Christ will be more and more at home in your hearts as you trust in him. May your roots go down deep into the soil of God's marvelous love. And may you have the power to understand, as all God's people should, how wide, how long, how high, and how deep his love really is. May you experience the love of Christ, though it is so great you will never fully understand it. Then you will be filled with the fullness of life and power that comes from God." (Ephesians 3:14–19 NLT)

If you don't want to be disappointed in life, receive the hope that comes from the assurance of God's love for you:

"And this hope will not lead to disappointment. For we know how dearly God loves us, because he has given us the Holy Spirit to fill our hearts with his love." (Romans 5:5 NLT)

Walk in faith upon what you know is true, what God has said, and what He's promised you.

2. God knows every detail of your life. There is NOTHING that God is not aware of. He knows every intricate detail of your life, from beginning to end, and He's not surprised by where you've been, what you've done, where you are, or where you're going. *He knows.* If He can keep the entire world in motion, don't you think He can manage your life? Why do we continually fail to realize this? Doubt creeps in amid pain and suffering—fear takes hold, and faith takes a back seat to our agony and we lose sight of the truth in Psalm 139:1–6:

> *"O LORD, You have searched me and known me. You know when I sit down and when I rise up; you understand my thought from afar. You scrutinize my path and my lying down, And are intimately acquainted with all my ways. Even before there is a word on my tongue, Behold, O LORD, You know it all. You have enclosed me behind and before, And laid Your hand upon me. Such knowledge is too wonderful for me; It is too high, I cannot attain to it."* (NASB)

Don't for a second believe that God has set the world in motion, but has let go of it … and that means *your* world.

> *"God's knowledge is linked to his sovereignty: he knows each thing, both in itself and in relation to all other things, because he created it, sustains it, and now makes it function every moment according to his plan for it (Ephesians 1:11). The idea that God could know, and foreknow, everything without controlling everything seems not only unscriptural but nonsensical."* —J. I. Packer, *Concise Theology: A Guide to Historic Christian Beliefs*

3. God is able. Why is it that we believe God can do some things, but not most? Why do we believe in some areas of life, but completely doubt Him in others? If we were walking in faith, *we wouldn't.* It's when we're questioning His power and presence that we should be alerted that our faith is failing—we can't walk by what we see. It's when we start questioning God that we should realize we've stepped out of our place and tried to take His. When we see *impossibilities*, God sees *opportunities* for miracles. Nothing is too difficult for Him and all things are possible when we allow Him to be who He is.

> *"Is anything too hard for the LORD?"* (Genesis 18:14 NLT)

> *"For nothing is impossible with God."* (Luke 1:37 NLT)

> *"Humanly speaking, it is impossible. But not with God. Everything is possible with God."* (Mark 10:27 NLT)

Don't miss that one word: EVERYTHING. It was obvious that the Israelites had no expectations of God parting the Red Sea—who would even think of such a thing? They knew they needed a miracle, but nothing within their human knowledge would have fathomed the parting of the sea that was before them. They learned what "everything" meant. We, too, need to grasp the reality that God is all powerful, capable of doing *anything* and *everything* to accomplish His will in our lives. Don't set limits on God, believe Him for the impossible, and watch Him work on your behalf as you stand at your Red Sea, paralyzed by fear. God will show up—then *your faith will take sight.*

> *"Faith is to believe what you do not see; the reward of faith is to see what you believe."* —St. Augustine

4. Trust God. We struggle to trust God. We want to, but fear gets the best of us, so we doubt. We believe God is good "sometimes," just not "all the time." Because He doesn't seem all that "good" when we're in financial distress, when our health is failing, when our family is falling apart, and pain and suffering lingers with no end in sight. We so easily lean on our own understanding, even though God has told us not to:

> *"Trust in the LORD with all your heart, and do not rely on your own understanding."* (Proverbs 3:5 NASB)

We have to choose to trust God rather than submit to fear.

"Fear is simply unbelief parading in disguise." —source unknown

If there was ever a promise that God knew we would need through the trials and tribulations, it was John 16:33 (NASB):

"These things I have spoken to you, so that in Me you may have peace. In the world you have tribulation, but take courage; I have overcome the world."

Courage. It's the *opposite* of fear. Merrian-Webster's online dictionary says it's the "ability to do something that you know is difficult or dangerous." A fuller definition says, "mental or moral strength to venture, persevere, and withstand danger, fear, or difficulty." Courage won't come easily, but through trusting in God's promises, it *will* come ... and your *fears* will give way to *faith*.

"Fear imprisons, faith liberates; fear paralyzes, faith empowers; fear disheartens, faith encourages; fear sickens, faith heals; fear makes useless, faith makes serviceable—and most of all, fear puts hopelessness at the heart of life, while faith rejoices in its God." —Harry Emerson Fosdick

Know that fear is what *brings about* courage. And as courage comes from trusting God, you can rely on the promises of God to help you overcome the gnawing and anxious feelings that come from being in fearful situations. Trust in God's promises to you, in order to overcome the fear factor that comes with faith:

*"Even though I walk through the darkest valley, **I will fear no evil**, for you are with me; your rod and your staff, they comfort me."* (Psalm 23:4 NIV; emphasis mine)

*"**Do not be afraid!** Be strong, and see how the Lord will save you today."* (Exodus 14:13 NLV; emphasis mine)

"Be strong and have strength of heart. **Do not be afraid** *or shake with fear because of them. For the Lord your God is the One Who goes with you. He will be faithful to you. He will not leave you alone."* (Deuteronomy 31:6 NLV; emphasis mine)

*"For I am the Lord your God Who holds your right hand, and Who says to you, '**Do not be afraid.** I will help you.'"* (Isaiah 41:13 NLV; emphasis mine)

"The Lord is my Light and my Salvation—whom shall I fear or dread? The Lord is the Refuge and Stronghold of my life— **of whom shall I be afraid?"** (Psalm 27:1 AMP; emphasis mine)

"Peace I leave with you. My peace I give to you. I do not give peace to you as the world gives. **Do not let your** *hearts be troubled or* **afraid.***"* (John 14:27 NLV; emphasis mine)

"The LORD *is my helper, so* **I will have no fear.***"* (Hebrews 13:6 NLT; emphasis mine)

The *fourth secret* of faith is: *choose faith instead of fear,* by trusting Him, even when you're doubting that you should.

5

TRUST GOD,
NO MATTER WHAT

You'd think we'd be able to trust in a God who controls, as Francis Chan points out in his video "Just Stop and Think," *"a giant ball that we're standing on that's spinning at a thousand miles an hour ... and while it's spinning, it's flying around the sun at sixty-seven thousand miles an hour!"* Funny how we can't seem to trust Him with the smaller things in life. Be certain, *trusting God* brings about miracles in your life. *Nothing* else will.

Trusting God allows you to walk upon dry land through a parted sea, even when you don't know what lies on the other side. It enables you to receive the Holy Spirit, receiving the fullness of God's glory throughout life. Trusting God allows you to endure pain and suffering, knowing that He has a good purpose for it all, even when you can't grasp any understanding of it all at the moment. And trusting God is only learned through crisis situations; unfortunately there's no other way. And that's the overall purpose for the Red Sea moments in your life. God wants you to know Him, to trust Him. *It's that simple.* He wants you to know Him so intimately that you know His heart well enough to make decisions throughout life that are pleasing to Him, in order to bring glory to His name.

You might not be able to understand God's plans for your life, and you may doubt His love for you, especially as your tears all but drown you, but if you need a miracle, you're going to have to trust God—*no matter what.*

> *"Trusting God completely means having faith that He knows what is best for your life. You expect Him to keep His promises, help you with problems, and do the impossible when necessary."*—Rick Warren

The first question that arises as we face our Red Sea is "why me?" We instinctively believe we're facing the trials of life all alone and fail to live in the truth of 1 Corinthians 10:13:

> *"No test or temptation that comes your way is beyond the course of what others have had to face. All you need to remember is that God will never let you down; he'll never let you be pushed past your limit; he'll always be there to help you come through it."* (MSG)

Nowhere in the Bible does God tell us that those who trust in Him will be spared the troubles of this world. In fact, He's told us just the opposite:

> *"In this world you will have trouble."* (John 16:33 NIV)

Don't get so overwhelmed with your circumstances that you miss the promise that follows that warning in John 16:33:

> *"But take heart! I have overcome the world."*

By definition, if Christ has overcome this world, then He's declaring He has "gained control of it." And if He's in control of this world, then He's in control of your world. Jesus's words can penetrate our doubt and disbelief as we struggle with the whole trust thing:

"Stop doubting and believe." (John 20:27 NIV)

It's a clear command. We've simply got to trust God and stop relying on *what we think we know.* We try to understand so that we can trust, but the truth is we don't understand and *we don't have to.*

We have God's word, His promises, to carry us through all that we can't understand in this life.

"The Bible is not supposed to make sense, it is supposed to make faith." —Kamran Karimi

No matter what we are facing, we will never find ourselves in a situation in which God has not provided a promise to help us through it. And when we're tested, when we have Red Sea moments in life, we have the opportunity to choose to believe God's promises and trust Him. We have to learn to apply the promises to our problems, being fully persuaded that God can and will do what He's promised. We have to learn to have child-like faith.

"Truly, I say to you, unless you turn and become like children, you will never enter the kingdom of heaven. Whoever humbles himself like this child is the greatest in the kingdom of heaven." (Matthew 18:2–4 ESV)

Trusting God means humbling ourselves and accepting what God has spoken in His word. His word is *His heart.* Our human instinct is to be self-sufficient. We think we can do life on our own, until we realize we can't and we lose sight that it's God who has provided the very air we breathe. Whether we realize it or not, we're dependent upon God for everything, *but we don't live like we are.* Children depend completely upon their parents or guardians to care for them. They know they can't care for themselves and they are well aware that they don't have the knowledge or resources to survive on their own. We, too, are to have that kind of dependence upon God, but we don't. And when life takes us into desperate situations, we forget that no matter what we do, we can't make miracles happen—only God can. And if God provided a way for us have eternal life, why wouldn't He also provide us everything we need to get us to that point?

> *"He who did not spare his own Son, but gave him up for us all—how will he not also, along with him, graciously give us all things?"* (Romans 8:32 NIV)

How can love be expressed in any greater way? An innocent life laid down, taking on our sin, past, present, and future, so that we might be free from the eternal consequences that sin brings with it. The heart of God contains a love that we will never fully understand, *yet we can know it,* and it's when we know God's heart that we can trust Him.

When life is going according to our plan, we assume it's going according to God's. We associate good things, blessings, the fulfillment of our desires as God's love. When we're filled with joy, we find it easy to believe God is good and that He loves us. But when life takes a tragic turn for the worse, we're not so sure that God is all that good. We lose our confidence in God's love for us and our faith gives way to doubt and despair.

Our definition of "good" is far different than God's. His ways are higher *and* better—we're just not sure we believe the better part when our family is falling apart, our home is in foreclosure, our health is failing, and the bills aren't getting paid. We tend to allow life to create our vision of God instead of *allowing God to develop our vision of life.* Our perspective can instantly change in our trial and we need to be stable in our understanding of God's heart.

What we believe about God will shape our attitudes, expectations, and actions throughout our lives. And without a foundation of faith that rests on the truth that "God is good," we're not standing on solid ground.

*"You are good and do **only** good."* (Psalm 119:68 NLT; emphasis mine)

David declared in his Psalm what he knew to be true about God's character, and so must we. Even when what God is doing doesn't seem good, or when it doesn't seem like he's doing anything at all, we need to stand firm in our faith—*no matter what.* When life isn't going according to our plans, we have a choice to make: we can question God's love and doubt His heart, or we can believe that God's love and the heart of who He is will transform our ashes to beauty, as He's promised He will:

*"To grant [consolation and joy] to those who mourn in Zion—to give them an ornament (a garland or diadem) of **beauty instead of ashes**, the oil of joy instead of mourning, the garment [expressive] of praise instead of a heavy, burdened, and failing spirit—that they may be called oaks of righteousness [lofty, strong, and magnificent, distinguished for uprightness, justice, and right standing with God], the planting of the Lord, that He may be glorified."* (Isaiah 61:3 AMP; emphasis mine)

What we believe about God's heart, and whether or not we trust it, has the power to change everything in our lives. Our view of God is vital and the foundation of our faith. Trusting God renders our trials powerless over us in day-to-day life. When we're faced with our trials and the Red Sea is raging, we shouldn't be asking, *"Where is God?"* but *"Where is my faith?"* If we're not looking to God, we're not expecting a miracle. Don't give up on your miracle. Resist the temptation to doubt. Your breakthrough will come. *The waters will part.* Stay focused on God's goodness; rest and be confident in His heart. It's your assurance in God's love, His heart, that will bring about confident expectation that your miracle is coming. So use this waiting place in life, as you stand with a raging sea in front of you, the enemy closing in behind you, nowhere to run and no place to hide, as an opportunity to stand still and seek the Lord. *Get to know His heart.*

The question you'll need to ask yourself as your heart is filled with fear is: "Do *you* know God's heart?" Do you know Him that intimately? Do you trust Him with *all of your heart,* instead of leaning unto your own understanding? Most of us don't, especially when life is falling apart at the seams. If you want to know God's heart, if you want to trust Him and have the kind of peace that comes with that, you're going to have to read His word. The Bible is His voice and it reveals His character.

You see, you can know *about* God without really knowing Him at all. And if we're to trust God with all of our heart, we're going to have to trust Him for temporal things *and* spiritual things. We're going to have to believe Him, from keeping the world in motion and supplying the adequate oxygen we breathe to providing the job we need to pay our bills. *He's sovereign.* And it's easy to trust Him when all is well, but it's much more difficult to trust Him in affliction. Through your doubt, trust that the size of your faith doesn't matter; rather, it matters that your heart is fully convinced of His unchanging love, mercy, and grace. We'll need to continually humble ourselves and acknowledge that God is God and we are not, quieting our hearts as we trust in God's faithfulness.

As we wrestle with the whole idea of trusting in a God we can't see, we find ourselves focusing on what we *do* see, and that's to our detriment. The basis for our trust in God must go deeper than our immediate circumstances and experiences. But *faith isn't that easy.*

We've heard, *"Life is hard, but God is good."* We fully believe the first part of that phrase. We're just not so sure about the second part. When our faith is walking by sight, we question and doubt and ask, *"If God is good, why is life hard?"* What we've missed in our faith, as we struggle to trust God, is that life is hard because we're constantly trying to do it in our own strength. Matthew 11:28–29 tells us exactly what to do when our burdens are heavy and we're too weak to carry on:

> *"Come to me, all of you who are weary and carry heavy burdens, and I will give you rest. Take my yoke upon you. Let me teach you, because I am humble and gentle at heart, and you will find rest for your souls."* (NLT)

Until God shows up, as we're weary and heavy-laden, we're going to need *"rest for our souls."* And as we're struggling to take another step of faith, for some reason, God tells us to take His *yoke* upon us. Once again, God isn't making sense, as it seems He's asking us to carry something more than what we're able to.

A yoke is the symbol of burdens, associated with oxen in a field; they take the yoke upon themselves and draw a plow or heavy load behind them. The invitation in Matthew 11:28–29 is a paradox and seeming contradiction that leads us into an examination of what we're to do when we're trusting God, too weary to carry on, and in need of His peace and rest until He blesses us with His presence and power.

First, in this Scripture, Jesus is inviting the weary and the heavy-laden. He isn't just talking about those who are tired. Not doing anything can make us tired; we don't need to exert ourselves to be tired. Weariness comes in all kinds of shapes and sizes, so when Jesus speaks of weariness, He's including every unsatisfied soul. No matter what it is that is making you weary, *come to Him.* Whoever you are, whatever you're going through, come to Jesus.

When you come to the Lord, it seems as though He's causing a greater burden than the one you brought to Him. He asks you to take His yoke upon you. A yoke is for two cattle in bearing one burden or drawing one load. Here, in this moment of overwhelming circumstances, burdens that are far too much for you to bear, Jesus says, "Set them aside and bear with Me 'divine burdens' for the sake of those who are lost." Jesus calls us to greater purposes, suffering for the sake of others, allowing *your pain to be someone else's gain.* He tells us to cease from our own works, to rest, to pause from everything we're trying to accomplish on our own and according to *our will.* He's asking us to grab hold of the vision of God's will and abandon our own ... and that changes everything.

Trusting God entails abandoning our self-seeking will and fully embracing His, in order to further His kingdom and bring about "on earth as it is in heaven."

> *"May your will be done on earth, as it is in heaven."*
> (Matthew 6:10 NLT)

If we can do that, allowing God to use our burdens in divine ways, we'll find miracles showing up in our lives as we find ourselves caught up in God's grace.

"The Will of God"

I WORSHIP thee, sweet will of God!
And all thy ways adore;
To every day I live, I seem
To love thee more and more.

Thou wert the end, the blessed rule
Of our Saviour's toils and tears;
Thou wert the passion of his heart
Those three and thirty years.

And he hath breath'd into my soul
A special love of thee,
A love to lose my will in his,
And by that loss be free.

I love to see thee bring to nought
The plans of wily men;
When simple hearts outwit the wise,
Oh, thou art loveliest then.

The headstrong world it presses hard
Upon the church full oft,
And then how easily thou turn'st
The hard ways into soft.

I love to kiss each print where thou
Hast set thine unseen feet;
I cannot fear thee, blessed will!
Thine empire is so sweet.

When obstacles and trials seem
Like prison walls to be,
I do the little I can do,
And leave the rest to thee.

I know not what it is to doubt,
My heart is ever gay;
I run no risk, for, come what will,
Thou always hast thy way.

I have no cares, O blessed will!
For all my cares are thine:
I live in triumph, Lord! for thou
Hast made thy triumphs mine.

And when it seems no chance or change
From grief can set me free,
Hope finds its strength in helplessness,
And gayly waits on thee.

Man's weakness, waiting upon God,
Its end can never miss,
For men on earth no work can do
More angel-like than this.

Ride on, ride on, triumphantly,
Thou glorious will, ride on!
Faith's pilgrim sons behind thee take
The road that thou hast gone.

He always wins who sides with God,
To him no chance is lost;
God's will is sweetest to him, when
It triumphs at his cost.

Ill that he blesses is our good,
And unbless'd good is ill;
And all is right that seems most wrong,
If it be his sweet will.

—Frederick William Faber (1814–63)

We need to fully understand that if we're going to trust
God, walking in His will, He's going to lead us into, or allow us

to venture into, situations where the burden is too heavy. It's a lesson of faith—realizing we can't do it alone, that we need God to not only lead and guide us, but at times, carry us. He's a ready help in times of trouble. Dare to believe what He's promised:

"God is our place of safety. He gives us strength. He is always there to help us in times of trouble." (Psalm 46:1 NIRV)

He keeps us safe, gives us strength, and ALWAYS provides the help. It may not come when we want it to or how we'd prefer, but what God's promised, *He will do.* God is telling you that whatever you're dealing with in life, if you'll ask Him to help you and pray for His strength, you can do anything because He's also promised in Philippians 4:13 that you can do ALL things through Christ. ALL things. Nothing is excluded from all. Nothing is left out of that equation, that promise; there's no end to it, nothing outside of it. All is all. Let *Him* be your all in all.

The Israelites stood at the Red Sea, angry with Moses and hostile toward God, questioning God's ways, paralyzed by fear, trying to figure out what *they were going to do.* And your life's situations, the trials you face, will instantly bring that very same question into your mind and torture your soul until you provide an answer: *"What are you going to do?"* Your only reply should be, *"I'm going to trust God."* Our shout should be one of confident faith: *"God, I trust in You. I don't know what You're doing, but I know You're working in my circumstances. I don't know how You're going to rescue me, but I know You will. I don't know when You'll show up, but I'm expecting You to. And in my faith, I stand firm upon the promises You've made, until you give my faith sight."*

Trusting God will not come easily. Don't allow yourself to be deceived that it will. But it's in understanding God's heart of boundless love and endless grace that will enable to you to take one more step of faith. So the *fifth secret of faith* is: make the decision to walk confidently in faith, trusting in God, through your doubts—*no matter what.*

6

SEE YOUR TRIAL
AS GOD DOES

God tells us that His thoughts and ways are *higher* than our own, and we can grasp that truth—we're just not sure they're *better*.

> *"'For my thoughts are not your thoughts, neither are your ways my ways,' declares the Lord. 'As the heavens are higher than the earth, so are my ways higher than your ways and my thoughts than your thoughts.'"* (Isaiah 55:8–9 NIV)

God has a *completely* different perspective, and we struggle continually to even get a glimpse of it. Our faith needs God's perspective, *not our own*, if we're to have any kind of victory in this life. Instead of walking in understanding, wisdom, and discernment, our hearts are blinded by the doubt and disbelief that come from prolonged unanswered prayers. When we must endure longer than we anticipated, we need to gain God's perspective because we can know God, understanding what He has said and done, but it's a spiritual perspective that helps us in understanding the whys, to the degree that God reveals those answers. In Psalm 103:7 (GOD'S WORD; emphasis mine) we read,

*"He let Moses **know his ways**. He let the Israelites **know the things he had done**."*

Trusting God allows us to understand life from God's perspective, and that enables us to reap the benefits of seeing our trials as God does. We are able to draw nearer to God and grow to love Him more as we see things from His perspective. We're able to walk in the truth that God is working all things for good (Romans 8:28) and that the tests and trials we're going through develop a persevering faith (James 1:3). We, just like Jesus, can look past the pain of our circumstances to the joy set before us (Hebrews 12:2).

Seeing life from God's perspective affects how we view all of life's aspects. It affects our values, expectations, priorities, and countless facets of life that we're not even aware of. We are well aware that life here is temporary, but we fail to grasp that life is a test of faith to develop our character. We can't see life through our own eyes, but through God's. Only *then* will our lives be transformed and renewed so that we might walk in the will of God and readily into the miracle that awaits us.

*"Don't copy the behavior and customs of this world, but **let God transform you** into a new person by changing the way you think. Then you will learn to know God's will for you, which is good and pleasing and perfect."* (Romans 12:2 NLT; emphasis mine)

Listen, you're not going to be able to instantly change your perspective, especially if you're faced with a Red Sea. And worry, which leads to fear, will be the first thing you'll need God to transform. We worry because we're unable to control the outcome of our situation and the what-ifs in life trap us into doubting God's presence and power. When we allow God's truth, His word, to penetrate our souls, as we trust in what He's promised, we'll find that our burdens are transformed into a bridge that takes us through the Red Sea.

We tend to look at adversity as a burden God has placed on us unjustly. Red Seas come in a variety of ways, but everyone faces Red Seas at one time or another. And it's easy to find your soul drowned out by the tears that flood your eyes and, all too often, become bitter and resentful toward a God who is supposed to love you. Your Red Sea moment is a critical moment in your life that will either be the burden that engulfs your faith or becomes the bridge that leads to your miracle. *Perspective changes everything.* So see your trial as God does—an opportunity to experience His presence and power in ways that will build a firm foundation of faith for the future.

When you're facing your Red Sea, waiting for God to show up, you'll need to see your fear through eyes of faith. We can learn how to do this best from Paul the Apostle. Paul wrote the majority of the New Testament through insights He derived through His losses and hardships. In Philippians 3:8–10 (NASB), Paul wrote, *"I count all things to be loss in view of the surpassing value of knowing Christ Jesus as my Lord . . . that I may know Him and the power of His resurrection and the fellowship of His suffer- ings, being conformed to His death."* And Paul didn't write this in the midst of great victory, but *in suffering.* You, too, can have this kind of faith, if you'll see it all through God's eyes instead of your own.

- **You can have peace and joy in your trials.** Paul assured us that we can have peace, even when life is filled with suffering. It can be difficult, at best, to find joy in our sorrows while we're experiencing them, but we can trust that God will bring about joy from sorrow through the promises He's made to us and His faithfulness throughout history. Paul wrote in Philippians 4:11–13 (NASB), *"I have learned to be content in whatever circumstances I am. I know how to get along with humble means, and I also know how to live in prosperity; in any and every circumstance I have learned the secret of being filled and going hungry, both of having abundance and suffering need. I can do all things through Him who strengthens me."* Not only did Paul teach us that we can be content and at peace, but we can have joy in the midst of our pain and suffering. And he didn't suggest that we rejoice in them, but that we rejoice in the Lord, knowing that if God is in control, we can be sure of the outcome of victory—we can count on God to work miracles, and we can rejoice in that assurance: *"Always be full of joy in the Lord. I say it again— rejoice!"* (Philippians 4:4 NLT)

- **Your strength will come through weakness.** We tend to look at adversity and injustices against us as those things that deplete our strength and faith, *and they do*. But if we're trusting in God, walking with Him in faith, we can see that God sees attacks against us, our weakness that comes from the sufferings of life, as something entirely different—*opportunities* for us to rely on His strength and power. It's how miracles happen. Paul writes in 2 Corinthians 12:9–10 (NLT), *" 'My grace is all you need. My power works best in weakness.' So now I am glad to boast about my weaknesses, so that the power of Christ can work through me. That's why I take pleasure in my weaknesses, and in the insults, hardships, persecutions, and troubles that I suffer for Christ. For when I am weak, then I am strong."*

- **You're not alone and God is faithful.** Each Red Sea you face in life gives you an opportunity to trust God in greater ways. Your *trial* is a *trail* to *trusting* God. See it as Paul saw His trials: an opportunity to trust in God's faithfulness. "*No test or temptation that comes your way is beyond the course of what others have had to face. All you need to remember is that God will never let you down; he'll never let you be pushed past your limit; he'll always be there to help you come through it*" (1 Corinthians 10:13 MSG).

- **God will use it *all* for good.** Maybe we can grasp most of what Paul is teaching us through our trials, but this one creates issues in our hearts. God's ways don't always seem to be better than our own, and we wrestle with trying to take God's place when we're suffering unduly. But we find throughout the Bible the evidence that God uses evil for good. He uses everything for His good purposes, *even when we lack understanding of how or when He'll do it.* We sometimes fail to clearly see that God will use our adversity as an effective message to have an impact for the kingdom of God. And though it's not the path we would have chosen, God knows that as others watch us persevere through our pain and suffering, walking firmly in faith, we fulfill His purposes for our lives in greater ways than we can ever comprehend. Read Paul's letter. God wants your sufferings in life to serve the same purpose—an eternal one:

"*I want to report to you, friends, that my imprisonment here has had the opposite of its intended effect. Instead of being squelched, the Message has actually prospered. All the soldiers here, and everyone else, too, found out that I'm in jail because of this Messiah. That piqued their curiosity, and now they've learned all about him. Not only that, but most of the followers of Jesus here have become far more sure of themselves in the faith than ever, speaking out fearlessly about God, about the Messiah.*

"It's true that some here preach Christ because with me out of the way, they think they'll step right into the spotlight. But the others do it with the best heart in the world. One group is motivated by pure love, knowing that I am here defending the Message, wanting to help. The others, now that I'm out of the picture, are merely greedy, hoping to get something out of it for themselves. Their motives are bad. They see me as their competition, and so the worse it goes for me, the better—they think—for them." (Philippians 1:13–15 MSG)

When your sufferings become a comfort to others, *"all things have worked together for good."* And although the miracle might not happen *to* you, it may just happen *through* you. So allow God to use your life—*you* may very well be someone's miracle they've been praying for, and your pain may be the path for that miracle to happen.

"All praise to the God and Father of our Master, Jesus the Messiah! Father of all mercy! God of all healing counsel! He comes alongside us when we go through hard times, and before you know it, he brings us alongside someone else who is going through hard times so that we can be there for that person just as God was there for us. We have plenty of hard times that come from following the Messiah, but no more so than the good times of his healing comfort—we get a full measure of that, too." (2 Corinthians 1:3–5 MSG)

Our Red Sea moments, and all the trials that follow, are meant to keep us humble and dependent upon God. Our trials are divinely designed to serve purposes that go beyond anything that we can understand, this side of heaven. Choose to see your trials as God does—*that's when miracles happen.*

No matter what you're facing, don't see your obstacles in any other way than through God's eyes. We have to remember that even when we don't have a vision of our future, *God does.* And more than likely we're not going to see the vision until God reveals it in His perfect time and in His perfect way, through His unlimited strength and resources. Just because we don't see anything happening doesn't mean God isn't working. Everything in our future, through our faith in God, is dependent upon how we see our trials.

If we want a clear and powerful lesson in seeing things as God sees them, even in the face of fear, we can go back to the account of the twelve spies, recorded in the book of Numbers, chapter 13.

One spy from each of the twelve tribes was sent by Moses into the land of Canaan, the promised land, for forty days in order to scout it out. What we find is that ten of the twelve spies lied about the land. They went back to Moses reporting that they couldn't take over the land because the people were fierce. They doubted God's abilities and resources to help them receive the promise he'd made them. It was due to their lack of faith in God, not seeing things as God saw them, that caused them to wander in the desert for forty years, killing most of that entire generation.

Later (Joshua 2), it was Joshua and Caleb who were the two spies who dared to believe God. And they were the only men from their generation that were permitted to go into the promised land after their wandering in the desert. Perspective changed everything—faith brought about the miracle of inhabiting the promised land.

How you see your trials and how you face your fears can, and will, determine the outcome of them. Obstacles, such as Red Seas, need not be reasons for discouragement. They should only be seen as extraordinary opportunities to encounter God's faithfulness. That's how God sees them. *Do you?* Maybe you want to believe that God will be enough in your times of need, but struggle with it all when He fails to show up *when you think He should.*

We want a God who shows up and all we have to do is believe. But sometimes we use faith to try and force God's hand because *we're not sure we approve of His will.* And when we don't believe God is doing His job, our whole perspective changes. Our vision gets blurred by our unmet needs and unanswered prayers. If God promises, "*The LORD will withhold no good thing from those who do what is right*" (Psalm 84:11 NLT), then why are we without a job, visiting a cancer center where a loved one waits to die, sitting opposite our wayward child with a glass boundary between us? Why are we living with an addict who won't seek help while our family falls to pieces? It sure seems as though God is withholding "good things." So what could be wrong? What is it we're doing that could be preventing our miracle?

- **We confuse our needs and wants.** When our needs are unmet and our desires unfulfilled, we need to ask God to examine our hearts to see if there is anything in it that offends Him. We need to ask God to sift our faith and help us to see what we truly need and what we're desiring that may not be in our best interest. Psalm 37:4 promises that God wants to fulfill the "desires of our hearts," but He's more interested in working out His purposes for our lives so that our lives will have eternal value. We need to pray diligently that God will change our desires so that they are in line within His will, so that Red Seas are parted.

- **We have not because we ask not.** Sometimes we simply forget to ask. We assume God knows our needs and we shouldn't have to tell Him. After all, in Matthew 6:8, He says that He knows what we need before we ask ... right? But God is after our relationship with Him and He wants *constant* communication. He wants you asking SPECIFICALLY for the miracle. Only then can you know for sure that it was God and not a coincidence. God assures us in His word, *"You don't have the things you want, because you don't pray for them. When you pray for things, you don't get them because you want them for the wrong reason—for your own pleasure"* (James 4:2–3 GOD'S WORD). We can't be afraid to ask God for the small miracles as well as the big ones. We need to walk in faith and obey exactly what Jesus instructed: *"Ask and it will be given to you; seek, and you will find; knock and the door will be opened to you"* (Matthew 7:7 NIV). We can't expect to receive miracles from God if we haven't asked Him for them. And when you ask ... don't doubt:

"Therefore I tell you, whatever you ask for in prayer, believe that you have received it, and it will be yours." (Mark 11:24 NIV)

"But when you ask him, be sure that your faith is in God alone. Do not waver, for a person with divided loyalty is as unsettled as a wave of the sea that is blown and tossed by the wind." (James 1:6 NLT)

• **We fail to wait on God.** We don't like God's watch. Most of the time it doesn't seem to be telling time. We pray for a miracle and things go from bad to worse. We get tired of waiting on Him to show up and we move ahead of His plan, only to find ourselves in a pit of despair far deeper than anything we could have ever imagined. We need to understand clearly that God doesn't work under pressure. If we'll trust in God's love for us, we can wait as long as it takes for God's perfectly timed arrival. His perfect plans are just that: *perfect.* So to second-guess God would only cause us to miss out on the miracle He's planned, and *no one wants to miss that.*

"The vision will still happen at the appointed time. It hurries toward its goal. It won't be a lie. If it's delayed, wait for it. It will certainly happen. It won't be late." (Habakkuk 2:3 GOD'S WORD)

- **We don't *seek first* ...** Let's face it, when there's a problem or crisis, we first try to solve it or remedy the situation. We forget to "seek first" God's kingdom and His righteousness. We've been clearly instructed in Matthew 6:33 (NLT):

"Seek the Kingdom of God above all else, and live righteously, and he will give you everything you need."

Such a simple equation, yet one our faith never seems to follow. If we'll seek God first, our trials won't become larger and larger to us; when we're seeing everything through God's eyes, trusting Him first and foremost, we find that *everything* is small to Him. We must never forget that He is able to do *"far more abundantly beyond all that we ask or think"* (Ephesians 3:20 NASB), so allowing Him to do what He does best—be God—gives Him the opportunity to hear our prayers and provide the miracle.

We can believe God for miracles, but until we trust in His sovereignty, we'll never have the peace we need to face our Red Seas. We need to be absolutely certain that God knows and God sees. We need to be assured that God is never almost sovereign.

Whether you like it or not, you're going to have to wait for your miracle, and you need the peace of God as you do. We can't allow doubt to get the best of us, creating uncertainty about God's power over what seems like an insurmountable circumstance. Although we can't see all that God sees, and we can't fully understand His ways, *we can trust them.* And the Bible tells us that God has ultimate authority. As we wait for our miracle, we're going to have to walk in faith and believe it.

"The LORD has made the heavens his throne; from there he rules over everything." (Psalm 103:19 NLT)

Everything. That means NOTHING happens apart from God's awareness, loving purposes, and control. We must learn to continually lay down our worries in light of this truth. And that's the *sixth secret* to faith: see your trial as God sees it—trusting in His sovereignty, His limitless power, His boundless love, and His endless grace ... and when you do, miracles *will* happen.

7

PRAISE GOD FOR THE PAST, PRESENT, AND FUTURE

When Red Seas get parted, they are often followed by multitudes looking on, stunned in disbelief, and paralyzed in awe by the miracle that was never expected and beyond imaginable. When the silence breaks, what follows is the instinct of *praise*. We're told that if we don't rejoice, even the *rocks* will cry out.

> *"'I tell you,' he replied, 'if they keep quiet, the stones will cry out.'"* (Luke 19:40 NIV)

Here's the hard truth about faith: maybe we need a Red Sea moment in life. Maybe we need to find ourselves upon our knees more often than we'd like. Perhaps one of the reasons we face Red Seas, whether by our own doing or by God's leading, is so that we can find a reason to praise Him. It's hard to ignore the countless praises that have come not only upon victory, but *within the pain and suffering*. That kind of faith, the faith that praises God before His power and presence are performed through miracles, is the kind of faith God's after in our hearts. Yet He knows that we need to experience the realization of His promises so that we can learn to praise. And all too often, that's going to require Him to put us in difficult, painful places, so that He can perform the miracle.

"He lets out His mercies to us for the rent of our praise, and is content that we may have the benefit of them so He may have the glory." —John Trapp

You see, when we see things from God's point of view, *praise* is the result. When we grab hold of God's promises in our lives, we are able to praise God for all He's done, is doing, and is yet to do. We can rejoice in His love and faithfulness for the past, present, and future.

Praise has its benefits in the midst of our trials of life. It helps us to focus upon God with little to no effort; it reminds us of God's sovereignty, magnifying God instead of our problems; it increases our faith, and fills our hearts with His joy as our praise paves the path to His awesome power in our lives.

And praise, just like everything else in faith, is a *choice*. It can come from experiencing a miracle, but more often than not, we're going to have to choose to praise God *before* the rocks cry out. We have a choice to dive into the depths of despair and discouragement or we can allow the place we find ourselves, upon our knees, to be holy ground on which we lift up praise to God.

If we want to understand how to praise God, we can look to Psalm 71 (NLT):

1 *O LORD, you are my refuge; never let me be disgraced.*

2 *Rescue me! Save me from my enemies, for you are just. Turn your ear to listen and set me free.*

3 *Be to me a protecting rock of safety, where I am always welcome. Give the order to save me, for you are my rock and my fortress.*

4 *My God, rescue me from the power of the wicked, from the clutches of cruel oppressors.*

5 *O LORD, you alone are my hope. I've trusted you, O LORD, from childhood.*

6 *Yes, you have been with me from birth; from my mother's womb you have cared for me. No wonder I am always praising you!*

7 *My life is an example to many, because you have been my strength and protection.*

8 *That is why I can never stop praising you; I declare your glory all day long.*

9 *And now, in my old age, don't set me aside. Don't abandon me when my strength is failing.*

10 *For my enemies are whispering against me. They are plotting together to kill me.*

11 *They say, "God has abandoned him. Let's go and get him, for there is no one to help him now."*

12 *O God, don't stay away. My God, please hurry to help me.*

13 *Bring disgrace and destruction on those who accuse me. May humiliation and shame cover those who want to harm me.*

14 *But I will keep on hoping for you to help me; I will praise you more and more.*

15 *I will tell everyone about your righteousness. All day long I will proclaim your saving power, for I am overwhelmed by how much you have done for me.*

16 *I will praise your mighty deeds, O Sovereign LORD. I will tell everyone that you alone are just and good.*

17 *O God, you have taught me from my earliest childhood, and I have constantly told others about the wonderful things you do.*

18 *Now that I am old and gray, do not abandon me, O God. Let me proclaim your power to this new generation, your mighty miracles to all who come after me.*

19 *Your righteousness, O God, reaches to the highest heavens. You have done such wonderful things. Who can compare with you, O God?*

20 *You have allowed me to suffer much hardship, but you will restore me to life again and lift me up from the depths of the earth.*

21 *You will restore me to even greater honor and comfort me once again.*

22 *Then I will praise you with music on the harp, because you are faithful to your promises, O God. I will sing for you with a lyre, O Holy One of Israel.*

23 *I will shout for joy and sing your praises, for you have redeemed me.*

24 *I will tell about your righteous deeds all day long, for everyone who tried to hurt me has been shamed and humiliated.*

From this Psalm we learn that the Lord:

- is a help in the present moment (verses 1 to 4),
- has helped in the past (verses 5 to 13),
- will help in the future (verses 14 to 21),
- will be praised (verses 22 to 24).

These are truths, promises ... it's up to us to truly believe them ... and we need to praise God, *regardless of our circumstances.* We need to realize that God is worthy to be praised *even if life is not.* Praising God is *not* optional.

Our highest calling is to praise God. Praise has powerful repercussions that affect this life and the one we're headed to. God has warned us, by the curse He pronounced over the children of Israel, that we are to praise Him or face the consequences of a life *without* praise. And a life without praise is a life without God's presence and power at work.

> *"If you do not serve the LORD your God with joy and enthusiasm for the abundant benefits you have received, you will serve your enemies whom the LORD will send against you. You will be left hungry, thirsty, naked, and lacking in everything."* (Deuteronomy 28:47–48 NLT)

You see, praising God has its purpose when you're praying for a miracle. When we praise God, we acknowledge that it is God who produces the blessings, who does the miracles, *not us.* God instructs us to praise Him, not for His benefit, but for our own. Praise keeps us humble and keeps us focused upon Him— the One who provides us with every good and perfect thing.

> *"And God will generously provide all you need. Then you will always have everything you need and plenty left over to share with others."* (2 Corinthians 9:8 NLT)

Our praise is a way to abound in faith. When our praise is present, we are walking in faith, and that pleases God.

> *"And now, just as you accepted Christ Jesus as your Lord, you must continue to follow him. Let your roots grow down into him, and let your lives be built on him. Then your faith will grow strong in the truth you were taught, and you will overflow with thankfulness."* (Colossians 2:6–7 NLT)

When you've prayed for a miracle, when you've faced a Red Sea and seen the waters parted as you walked across on dry ground, it's *easy* to praise God—it's a natural response to a miracle. Praising God when the waters aren't parting and the enemy is closing in doesn't come naturally at all. Yet we need faith to please God, and praise increases our faith. So we're going to have to choose to praise God, even when nothing within us wants to.

When we focus on our problems, instead of praising God, we become prideful, self-centered, and consumed with doing things our way. Praise changes all of that and is an act of faith that is an outward declaration that we acknowledge God is on His throne. Praise turns our hearts toward God and allows our prayers to move His.

Praise has its benefits. So if we're looking for a *payoff* to our *praise*, we can look to God's *promises* once again:

- **Praise gives us peace.** It's when we're consumed with fear that we simply need to say a prayer of praise so that God's power can bring about miracles. And one miracle in our Red Sea moment is having the peace of God keeping our heart and mind through it all.

  "Don't worry about anything; instead, pray about everything. Tell God what you need, and thank him for all he has done. Then you will experience God's peace, which exceeds anything we can understand. His peace will guard your hearts and minds as you live in Christ Jesus." (Philippians 4:6–7 NLT)

Everything we pray should *begin* with praise and *end* with it. It's the living proof that our faith is confident in God's faithfulness.

- **Praise strengthens us.** We need to look no further than the life of the Apostle Paul to understand how praise in the midst of suffering can alter our perspective. Praise builds us spiritually and helps us to see our Red Seas as God sees them. When Paul was faced with unending, unimaginable suffering, He looked to God and the spiritual side of things.

Praise pushes us out of the pit of despair and into God's powerful hands.

When Paul and Silas found themselves in prison, they chose to do something profound—praise God at *midnight*. When all hope seemed gone, in the darkness of midnight, Paul and Silas sang praises to God:

> *"Around midnight Paul and Silas were praying and singing hymns of praise to God. The other prisoners were listening to them. Suddenly, a violent earthquake shook the foundations of the jail. All the doors immediately flew open, and all the prisoners' chains came loose.*
>
> *"The jailer woke up and saw the prison doors open. Thinking the prisoners had escaped, he drew his sword and was about to kill himself. But Paul shouted as loudly as he could, 'Don't hurt yourself! We're all here!'*
>
> *"The jailer asked for torches and rushed into the jail. He was trembling as he knelt in front of Paul and Silas. Then he took Paul and Silas outside and asked, 'Sirs, what do I have to do to be saved?'*
>
> *"They answered, 'Believe in the Lord Jesus, and you and your family will be saved.' They spoke the Lord's word to the jailer and everyone in his home.*
>
> *"At that hour of the night, the jailer washed Paul and Silas's wounds. The jailer and his entire family were baptized immediately. He took Paul and Silas upstairs into his home and gave them something to eat. He and his family were thrilled to be believers in God."* (Acts 16:25–34 GOD's WORD)

As Paul and Silas praised God, others listened. (Be aware that others are watching you and your life as well. If you say you have faith, does your life prove you do? When you're faced with a Red Sea moment in life, do others see your fear or the face of your God?) Not only were Paul and Silas set free by the earth-quake that broke their chains, but the jailer and his family were saved, given eternal life, because the jailer had witnessed the praises of God work a miracle. Sometimes that's all it takes for someone to believe, and sometimes that's the *only* reason you're going through pain and suffering.

When all of your strength is spent and you're at the end, know that praise will carry you in your faith.

"... the joy of the LORD is your strength!" (Nehemiah 8:10 NLT)

Praise releases the power of God and increases our faith in the face of fear. Our life should be a life of praise; it's our way of building an intimate relationship with God, which we desper-ately need if we're ever to witness miracles in our lives.

"Therefore, let us offer through Jesus a continual sacrifice of praise to God, proclaiming our allegiance to his name." (He-brews 13:15 NLT)

Sometimes we'll see praise as more of a sacrifice, and Hebrews 13:15 gives us that awareness—as we walk in faith, reckoning our praise as the promise of God's power, we struggle with the choice of praising God when bad things happen. Our feelings can fall in the way of our faith. Are we supposed to thank God when tragedy strikes, when fear consumes us in our Red Sea moment? We learn, through our faith, that it's not about praising God *for* them, but *in* them, realizing that even when we can't understand His ways, *we can trust them.* If we wait until we feel like praising God, we seldom will. It means we can remain joyful, praising God, no matter what obstacles in life we face, because we know the end of the story—we must make the choice to believe the second part of John 16:33 (NLT):

"I have overcome the world."

It's in the midst of fear that our faith can rise up and choose to praise God in words similar to those in Psalm 34:1–7 (NASB):

I will bless the LORD at all times;
His praise shall continually be in my mouth.
My soul makes its boast in the LORD;
The humble will hear it and rejoice.
Oh, magnify the LORD with me,
And let us exalt his name together!
I sought the LORD, and he answered me
And delivered me from all my fears.
They looked to him and were radiant,
And their faces will never be ashamed.
This poor man cried, and the LORD heard him
And saved him out of all his troubles.
The angel of the LORD encamps around those who fear Him,
And delivers them.

Praising God continually magnifies God instead of our problems, and that changes everything. Victory comes through praise and brings about God's miracles in our lives.

If you want God to bless you, try blessing Him first by praising Him with all your heart and soul.

"Bless the LORD, O my soul: and all that is within me, bless his holy name. Bless the LORD, O my soul, and forget not all his benefits: Who forgiveth all thine iniquities; who healeth all thy diseases; Who redeemeth thy life from destruction; who crowneth thee with loving-kindness and tender mercies; Who satisfieth thy mouth with good things; so that thy youth is renewed like the eagle's. The LORD executeth righteousness and judgment for all that are oppressed." (Psalm 103:1–6 KJV)

So the *seventh secret* to faith is: praise God at *all* times and in *all* ways. And as you praise the God of miracles, you'll need to do one more thing: *believe*. Before a miracle ever happens, you must believe. God's ways say that *believing is seeing*. We need not to only believe that God is *able* to work a miracle in our lives, but that He *will* do it. Jesus commanded Thomas, and His command to us is no different:

"Stop doubting and believe." (John 20:27 NIV)

Miracles happen every day. *Stop doubting* that they can happen to *you*. Faith goes beyond the reach of proof, *so stop reaching* ... just *choose* to have faith. And when you're tempted to believe that God has missed the miracle moment, know that it's *never* too late for God to show up.

"Have faith in God and wait; Although he linger long, He never comes too late. He never comes too late, He knoweth what is best: Vex not thyself in vain; Until he cometh, rest."
—Bradford Torrey

God knows *when* you need a miracle and *how* to bring it about. Leave the *details* in His hands and fully trust your heart to His.

As you stand before the Red Sea in your life, tempted to fear, remember that you're on the verge of a miracle—it's only a matter of *God's perfect timing*. Just stand still, in faith, knowing that God hears your prayers and will answer them according to His perfect plans and purposes for your life. Don't get in a power struggle with God—*He always wins*. Don't have expectations about the details of the miracle you pray for, but simply expect God to show up. Choose to trust, pray, and praise—*that's how your miracle will happen.*

"The Red Sea Place"

Have you come to the Red Sea place in your life
Where in spite of all you can do,
There is no way out.
There is no way back.
There is no other way but through.
Then wait on the Lord with a trust serene
'Til the night of your fear is gone;
He will send the winds,
He will heap the floods,
When He says to your soul, "Go on."

And His hand will lead you through—
clear through
Ere the watery walls roll down.
No foe can reach you,
No wave can touch,
No mightiest sea can drown.
The tossing billows may rear their crests,
Their foam at your feet may break;
But over their bed you shall walk dry shod
In the path that your Lord will make.

—Annie Johnson Flint

(Continued from copyright page)

ABOUT THE AUTHOR

Cherie Hill is the founder of ScriptureNow.com, a global ministry that brings the blessing of Scripture to more than thirty countries. Cherie takes joy in helping others explore the promises and blessings found within God's Word. With a BA in psychology and biblical counseling training through the American Association of Christian Counselors, she writes for several online Christian magazines and counsels through various radio programs. When not writing or speaking, she commits her time to her church and various nonprofit organizations.